"Pure religion is looking aft
near and dear to the heart o
the church to step up and ste

—Mark Batterson
Lead Pastor, National Community Church
New York Times Best Selling Author

"Fostering Jesus is a comprehensive work. It informs, educates, and fuels the soul. The content should not be taken lightly; rather, it provides a guide for a follower of Christ to become involved in caring like Jesus did, with mind, body, and soul."

—Dr. Sharen E. Ford
Director of Foster Care & Adoption Advocacy, Focus on the Family

"For too long the church has stood by while the foster system in America has deteriorated. Now is the time for the church to step up. Pastor Bob's story will inspire and empower you and your church to do just that in a way that will impact your community and the lives of hurting children for Christ."

—Hanna Hurst
U.S. Missionary and U.S. Chaplain to Orphan Care

"Dr Bob Griffith has provided an outstanding resource on foster care. Combining biblical truths with his personal experiences, *Fostering Jesus* presents a compelling case for why the church should be engaged in foster care ministry. The church is uniquely positioned to provide the answer for the foster care crisis in America."

—Doug Clay
General Superintendent of the Assemblies of God

"Foster care ministry is at the heart of the gospel! Dr. Bob Griffith's book is an important resource for caring pastors and churches in this cause. I have invested most of my thirty-eight years of credentialed ministry in reaching, redeeming, and raising up the next generation for Jesus Christ, especially the more vulnerable ones who God so jealousy loves. A few years ago, 47 percent of pastors in a major denominational national study said they would make foster care ministry a top three priority in their church if they just knew what to do and how to do it! This book informs what and how!"

—Jay Mooney
Chief Ministries & Resources Officer, Assemblies of God National Office

"Dr. Bob Griffith calls readers to 'join us in the journey of helping vulnerable children today and not waiting for tomorrow!' Everyone needs to read *Fostering Jesus: Answering the Call to Foster Care in the Home and Church*. It challenges us to answer James 1:27—helping the widows and the orphans. Through real systems, scholarly research, and solutions it provides guidance for how churches can be the heroes in their communities by participating in foster care ministry."

—Dr. Kent Ingle
President, Southeastern University
Author of *9 Essentials of Enduring Leadership and Framework Leadership*

"Growing up, over a twenty-year period, my brothers and I had eighty different foster brothers and sisters live with us. My parents' mission was simply to show these children the love of Jesus and the love of a family—no matter how long they were with us. Now as a pastor, I see the need for people like my mom and dad who will open up their heart and their homes as large as ever. I believe Bob's book is incredibly important to help Christians consider this beautiful responsibility as he gives clear action steps to get involved. As you read it, I pray you will see that we can love the foster children in our communities by sharing our homes and opening our hearts to them and living out our faith in a much-needed way."

—Rob Ketterling
Lead Pastor, River Valley Church
Author of *Speed of Unity*

"America is facing a crisis. Children across the nation are at risk because homes are fracturing. Consequently, the foster care system is being overwhelmed. Dr. Bob Griffith's timely book, *Fostering* Jesus, is a call to believers to demonstrate the compassion of Christ. The book is both practical and inspiring. This book is definitely worth your time!"

—Hal Donaldson
President & Founder, Convoy of Hope

"People in social services and in the legal system know that across the United States hundreds of thousands of abused and neglected children are in need. These children need loving foster parents and foster parents need support. How can your church answer the call? In this book, Dr. Bob Griffith offers a roadmap for how your church, your pastors, your leaders, and you can step up. Open your homes to foster children. Open your hearts to foster parents. Transform the foster system in your community. You have the will; let Pastor Griffith show you the way."

—Michael D. Graveley
District Attorney, Kenosha County, Wisconsin

"Jesus places the child at the center of His Kingdom message, and James—His brother—defines pure religion as care for orphans and widows. Bob and Wendy Griffith have embodied this in their lives, and now they provide an accessible rationale for fostering and adopting. Filled with personal testimonies, biblical insights, and practical pathways, this book is a prophetic gift to the church. Everyone who wishes to truly follow the teachings of Jesus should buy it, read it, and live it."

—Dr. Robby Waddell, PHD
Professor of New Testament and Early Christianity
at Southeastern University
Lead Pastor of Oasis Community Church

"Dr. Griffith's book is an eye-opening and informative book that delves deeply into the U.S. foster care crisis and why the Christian Church is an integral part of the solution. The extensive research and thoughtful analysis bring to light the challenges and opportunities faced by foster children and their caregivers and how every Christ-follower has a role in changing the way we care for vulnerable children and families in the U.S. This book is a must-read for anyone interested in understanding the complexities of foster care and for those who want to make a positive impact in the lives of vulnerable children and their families."

—Bill Hancock
Chief Strategy Officer of Blue Ocean Ventures Management
Founder and Former CEO of FaithBridge Foster Care

"Dr. Bob Griffith brings healing and hope to the most vulnerable. His inspiring passion will challenge and encourage you to make a difference. I recommend you read with an open heart as you are prepared to implement ministry to those who need it most."

—Dr. Alan Bixler
Executive Director—COMP*ACT* Family Services
National Director of the Assemblies of God Foster Care Network

"Pastors Bob and Wendy Griffith served on our team for more than a dozen years. Their passion for children is not a story; it is their life. In this book you will find not only an accounting of their personal journey but also the 'how-to' that makes it doable for you and me. At the heart of it is their Jesus-drive to give every child what he or she deserves: a family."

—Kevin Taylor
Lead Pastor—Journey Church, Kenosha, Wisconsin

"Bob has taken the time to give us a biblical and practical view of foster care. His love for the Word of God and the neglected and abused children of our society have led him to write a unique and ministry-provoking book. He starts with Jesus in a way most of us have not considered and then ends up with us. In addition to pastoring a successful church in the greater Washington DC area, Bob is a member of the Assemblies of God Foster Care Network. He has something to say that every Christian needs to hear. Don't overlook this book. Don't overlook the call of Jesus to minister to children.

—Rick DuBose
Assistant Superintendent of the Assemblies of God

Dr. Bob Griffith is a trusted friend who is absolutely absorbed with finding God solutions for the growing numbers of vulnerable children around the world. In this book, you will learn of the proven solutions that he and his wife have developed to help support foster care efforts from their personal and organizational leadership experience.

—Rich Wilkerson
Lead Pastor - Trinity Church

There are few pastors in the world like Dr. Bob Griffith that understand the church's biblical mandate to care for children, youth, and families involved in foster care. He truly lives out James 1:27 in searching for the distress of his community and then positions his church to be the gospel focused solution to that distress!

—Eric Porter
Founder and CEO – Backyard Orphans

Fostering Jesus

Answering the Call to Foster Care in the Home and Church

DR. BOB GRIFFITH

WITH REV. WENDY A. GRIFFITH

WestBow Press books may be ordered through booksellers or by contacting:

WestBow Press
A Division of Thomas Nelson & Zondervan
1663 Liberty Drive
Bloomington, IN 47403
www.westbowpress.com
844-714-3454

ISBN: 978-1-6642-9947-4 (sc)
ISBN: 978-1-6642-9949-8 (hc)
ISBN: 978-1-6642-9948-1 (e)

Library of Congress Control Number: 2023909447

Print information available on the last page.

WestBow Press rev. date: 7/13/2023

CONTENTS

DEDICATION

I dedicate this project to my wife, Wendy,
for having the vision to care for foster children when I did not.
She is a leader with vision for the potential our family has
to impact the world and how the church can do the same.
She dreams big about what is possible and desires to
see God glorified through those dreams. She makes
me a better husband, father, pastor, and friend.
Ministry is about teamwork, and God gave me the best teammate
I could ever hope for in this journey of faith.

FOREWORD

In 2008, just three months after I birthed our first child, our first foster child joined our family. He was a charming eight-year-old … and we were his seventh home in three years. I worked in social services, and my husband worked in an underserved school where many kids were foster children. We felt equipped and capable of being a Christ-centered, loving home for kiddos who needed one.

Six foster children and another birth child later, we realized how ill-equipped we were! As the first foster family in our church, we lacked community. But as our friends watched us take in kids, *they* also began to! Soon, our church had to adjust to the needs of foster families—stretching beyond comfort zones and into faith walks. So many churches still lack support and community for families like ours. It's essential for the body of Christ to welcome these social orphans and learn to love them as God so radically loves His own "grafted-in" children.

Little did we realize how much this journey of "caring for orphans and widows" would transform our lives. We thought we were giving the *kids* a gift, but God was giving *us* gifts, too. These gifts came through trial and fire but resulted in knowing God as an adoptive Daddy who loves His children unconditionally. I now better understand the tremendous gift of my *own* adoption into the family of God in a humbling and profoundly grateful way.

I cannot even begin to imagine fostering and adopting without Jesus. He's our model, He's our ever-present help, and He's our anchor. He plans to prosper us and our children, to give us a hope and a future. He is trustworthy. Yet so many believers stay in the "safety" of the comfortable, never getting to experience the adrenaline and transformation of living His miracles.

That's why I love this book. *Fostering Jesus: Answering the Call to Foster Care in the Home and Church* is a call to action. It's an invitation to participate with God's beating heart for these children, to *live* the heart of the gospel. We've let the government fail at raising these kids for too long. Yep, it's hard. So hard. But in the hard, we experience God's strength in our weakness, His miracles in the messes, and His presence in pain. We get to trade mourning for dancing and sorrow for joy. We get to model what it is to need Jesus to our precious children.

Dr. Bob Griffith and Rev. Wendy Griffith bravely hold up the reality of our nation ... homes are broken, and kids need loving homes—Spirit-filled homes.

Don't read this book if you like living a comfortable, safe, risk-free "faith."

Through their own firsthand story and numerous interviews and studies, the Griffiths provide real systems, scholarly research, and solutions used over a decade to help churches be lights in their community through foster care ministry. They offer a positive message about foster care, encouraging pastors, church leaders, and Christians who want to be part of the solution. They answer the tough questions about why God wants us to help children in foster care, why foster care should be a ministry in the church and how to do it successfully, how foster care can help *grow* the church, and what you can do to help—even if you can't bring a child into your home.

I *know* God is calling His people to join His mission. I'm so grateful for the chorus of voices, like the Griffiths, rising to bring attention to this issue. I am inspired by their work, not simply to speak the truth but also to personally live it. Don't read this book if you like living a comfortable, safe, risk-free "faith." These words will call you into the actual heart of God, and you won't be the same. Let's link arms and care for these orphans together.

—Marcy Pusey, CRC, CTRP-C

Best Selling Author:
Reclaiming Hope: Overcoming the Challenges of Parenting Foster and Adopted Children,

Parenting Children of Trauma: The Foster-Adoption Guide to Understanding Attachment Disorder,

Speranzcya's Sweater: A Child's Journey through Foster Care and Adoption
(Two-Time) TEDx Speaker
Foster-Adoptive Mama

PREFACE

The story of this book begins in our home and tells the story of our lived experience of walking out what the Apostle James calls "true religion" (Jas 1:27). My wife, Wendy, and I have six children. Four of our children, we adopted; of those, three were in foster care. Our story is one of loss, redemption, and miraculous conformation to what God wanted to take place through us.

Beyond our story, though, this book has emerged from our desire to encourage others to join us in this journey of helping vulnerable children *today* and not waiting for *tomorrow*. Foster care aligns with the mission of God as seen in Isaiah 1:17, Acts 6, Romans 8, and James 1:27. The New Testament Church has a history of leading the way with innovative solutions to rescue orphans.

When I asked local county officials in the judicial, legal, and social services sector how the church could help with foster care, they agreed that recruiting and supporting foster parents were the two largest needs. In response to this, and as the heart of my doctoral research, I established and evaluated[1] a foster family support program at Journey Church, a large church in Kenosha, Wisconsin, where I served at the time as an executive pastor. As a result, we saw families in our church step out in faith to foster children, which fed into a movement within this congregation and city. The results were exciting to see! After starting a foster family support system in our church, 30 percent of all the foster families in the county, attended the church.

This book tells this story. It provides real systems, scholarly research, and solutions used over ten years to help churches be heroes in their community through foster care ministry. It is for all Christ-followers (from congregants to church leaders) who want to help vulnerable children in their neighborhoods. To access the full research project, see the following link: https://firescholars.seu.edu/dmin/4/

ACKNOWLEDGMENTS

I want to thank Dr. Kent Ingle, the President of Southeastern University, for always believing in me. He is someone who sees the best in others and connects them with what they need to succeed in accomplishing their divine design. He is a great leader and a true friend.

In addition, I want to thank Pastor Rick DuBose, the Assistant Superintendent of the Assemblies of God, for his leadership and for allowing me to serve in the historic process of creating a National Foster Care Network (www.agfostercare.network) that seeks to advance the principles in this book throughout our entire county. His heart, leadership, and vision have inspired me and bring me hope that together, the churches of America can serve the vulnerable and participate in revival.

I would also like to thank Ray Knight, President of 1HOPE TOGETHER, a 501C(3) organization (www.1hope.community). I founded this organization in 2018 in partnership with Pastor Kevin Taylor of Journey Church, Kenosha, Wisconsin. Under the leadership of Ray Knight, it has continued to grow! Today, 1HOPE TOGETHER is now supporting more foster families than ever before as they partner with churches in their city from various denominations to answer the call of caring for the vulnerable.

INTRODUCTION

A Crisis and the Answer

America has a crisis in foster care, and the Christian community is the answer. Serving foster children is at the very heart of the gospel. Those who do serve foster children display God's glory and are recognized by the community as true heroes. As Judge Jason A. Rossell of Kenosha County Circuit Court affirms, "Other than recruiting more foster families, the greatest way churches can help is to support the foster parent." District Attorney Michael Gravely in Kenosha, Wisconsin echoes this support for foster care: "Foster parents are heroes. What they do is heroic every day. The number one way that churches can help is to support foster parents as they care for the most vulnerable children in our city."

A Unique Approach

This book presents a unique approach to America's foster care crisis. Given that of Wendy and my six children, four are adopted (three of whom were in foster care), we are *living this out with real world stories*—our own stories and those of others.

We also uniquely present in this book a *positive message* about foster care—not a behind the scenes look at all of what is hard with fostering children, but rather, we provide encouragement to those Christians on the fence who say they want to foster but are still waiting to decide. Thirty-eight percent of Christians surveyed say they want to foster, but only 1 percent of those do. Therefore, this book speaks to the 37 percent in that gap. The message of James 1:27, to care for "the orphans ... in their distress" is a command for 100 percent of Christians. This book spotlights the 'orphans'—called foster children—in every community. Though not everyone is called to bring a child into their home, everyone can do *something*. Thus, this book speaks to all 100 percent.

Third, this book provides a *unique approach to biblical church growth* in that it answers the *how* question for pastors and church leaders who want to do something big in their community to change their city in the name of Christ but don't know where to start. Many churches need to change their reputation in the community and break negative stereotypes after years of inward ministry and church decline. This approach spotlights a top need in every community that is close to the heart of God and that is easy to get off the ground. Surveys show that 47 percent of pastors would put foster care in the top three of their church vision goals if they only knew how.

Forty-seven percent of pastors would put foster care in the top three of their church vision goals if they only knew how.

The exciting news is that more and more Christians are answering the call to help vulnerable children. For example: the Assemblies of God (AG) has gotten behind this mission and has committed to living out the heart of the gospel through foster care. The AG national office has declared foster care a target issue to address in the coming years through the 12,000 churches in its network. The AG national women's ministries department has also picked up this issue as well. Additionally, a non-denominational rally in Orlando, Florida called "The Send" drew tens of thousands of Christians from around the country in 2019 and picked foster care as the issue they wanted to impact the most.

Finally, very few books actually offer a *foster care ministry plan for the church*, which this book does. When you search for the phrase, "foster care ministry," only a handful of books show up, and only a few speak to the issue. There is growing momentum for this topic in the country. Doors for international adoption have been closing, and people are searching for additional outlets to help orphans. Churches have historically focused on adoption, but adoption is the end of the cycle after all other efforts fall short. Foster care serves as a step before adoption, when church doors are open to help with discipleship and mentoring. The church world is starting to see foster care as a new area of ministry opportunity before the final adoption step, and this book can provide the help necessary to make a clear plan for the way forward.

For Whom is This Book Written?

This book is specifically for five segments of the community who want to participate in the heart of the gospel—pastors, church leaders, Christians wanting to foster children, Christians wanting to help in other ways, and those who want to do something that can directly prevent human trafficking.

- **Pastors** – Local pastors are called and excited about growing their church influence for the glory of God. However, they often do not have the time to launch another ministry or the budget to fund something new. The concept of being a missional church is commonly held by pastors everywhere, but they often appreciate some additional ideas on how to address the needs of the community they love so much. This book can help a pastor be the visionary leader their community is looking for. It can give their community hope that one of its biggest pain points could receive real help. This book positions local pastors to empower their congregation to make an impact no matter what size church they lead.

- **Church Leaders** – Similar to pastors, many volunteer church leaders care about this issue but don't know how to start a ministry in their church or approach their local community leadership to help solve foster care needs. This book gives them hope and a plan.
- **Christians Who Want to Foster a Child** – Many Christians have thought about fostering before but hesitate until they learn more or watch a friend do it successfully. This book tells those success stories and encourages Christians to take the next step.
- **Christians Who Can't Foster a Child but Want to Do Something to Help** – Congregations are full of people who can't foster or don't want to right now. These individuals are, however, interested in helping foster children *somehow* but just don't know *how*. This book offers a way for the average church goer to be a hero to foster children by supporting the foster parents who care for them every day.
- **Christians Wanting to Prevent Human Trafficking**: Foster care serves as a direct prevention to human trafficking. This is important because few ways exist to volunteer in the cause against human trafficking, but foster care has many ways a volunteer can participate. Foster care can mobilize large numbers of volunteers in efforts to prevent human trafficking.

In the chapters that follow, this book essentially answers the questions asked by these audiences relative to

1. why God wants them to help children in foster care,
2. why foster care should be a ministry in the church and how to do it successfully,
3. how foster care can help grow the church, and
4. if one can't foster a child, then what can they do to help?

To fully answer those questions, this book is divided into five Parts.

Part One (chapters 1-5) begins with our family's **personal** foster care and adoption story and the stories of four other couples.

Part Two (chapters 6-9) identifies the biblical mandate and justification for adoption and foster care. Specifically, chapter 6 examines how God compassionately cares for the marginalized, seeking to rescue the quartet of the vulnerable (poor, widow, orphan, foreigner)—and how He calls His people to do likewise. Chapter 7 describes the Spirit's empowerment available for all believers to care for orphans, chapter 8 considers the call of James 1:27 to care for orphans, and chapter 9 provides a pneumatology of foster care and adoption, specifically looking at Paul's understanding of the "spirit of adoption."

Part Three (chapters 10 and 11) will help you gain context with respect to the discussion about foster care and adoption by looking at the historical status of orphans, examining specifically how both society/the state and the church have attempted to respond to orphaned children throughout history and how these methods compare. Such a comparison will help identify the goals and expectations of a church-based response to foster care and inform the reader as to conversations that have been taking place on this topic for generations.

Part Four (chapters 12-14) looks at the contemporary approach of the Christian Church to foster care (chapter 12), specifically utilizing the foster family support model. Chapters 13 and 14 describe a pilot project I conducted establishing a foster family support program for a one-year implementation at Journey Church in Kenosha, Wisconsin. I first examine the steps we took to measure the *need* for our proposed support efforts and then describe the *evaluation* conducted following the implementation. I look at which support activities were most valued by foster families, which brought them the greatest satisfaction, and which failed to achieve that outcome. These measurement data provided the wisdom and insight needed for leaders to make better decisions about this ministry and gauged the level of foster family intent to continue with foster care in the next twelve months.

May God bless you as you read our stories, hear the cry of God's heart throughout Scripture, and embrace exciting new ways forward to walk in obedience to what He is calling you to do.

PART ONE

Saying Yes to Foster Care: Five Stories

Jesus told stories. They make things clear. They speak to our heart. Our stories are testimony to what God has done and is doing in the lives of people. We tell stories to give glory to God and build up the faith of those around us.

The first story in Part One is my testimony as the author. It is the story of how God made His plan clear to me over a period of time. Sometimes, it takes that long for us to recognize what God is doing in our lives and finally come into alignment with it. That was my story. I said no to fostering a child until I gave God a small opportunity to make it clear to me that this was, in fact, His plan. And he did!

The remaining stories were written by my wife, Pastor Wendy Griffith. She built relationships with each of these families and was impacted by their lives. She interviewed each family and captured the essence of what they felt was most important to know about their foster parent journey. Each story will speak to you in a different way, but all of them will make you better!

"As iron sharpen iron, so one person sharpens another" Prov 27:17 (NIV)

As we tell our stories of love lived out, we encourage and inspire each other to be our very best for the Lord.

CHAPTER 1

Bob and Wendy

The following story is my testimony as the author of this book. It is Wendy and my story and demonstrates how far God will go in a person's life to help vulnerable children. For us, he took down every mountain we saw in the way until the ground was flat and all we had to do walk forward.

Jonah was told to go to Nineveh, but he did not want to go, for fear held him back. The Israelites were also afraid when they found themselves ready to enter the Promised Land because the native people looked taller, stronger, and very dangerous! Moses, too, was afraid of the challenges ahead because he knew he would have to face Pharaoh when acting as the liberating agent for God's people. His calling appeared difficult, but that was God's plan.

In these and other scenarios throughout Scripture, God had a redemptive plan He needed carried out, but those He selected often resisted because the plan seemed too hard, and the cost seemed too high. They simply did not think they could do it without great pain. They felt the odds were too great and that the suffering would not be worth the reward. Thankfully, the Bible contains examples of how these people realized God's plan and often became catalysts for His redemptive work.

God's redemptive story continues in our world today as He seeks to save those who are marginalized, weak, and unable to provide for themselves. Orphans are one such people group who need saving all around the world, but who will save them? Who will step up to care for them and invite them into their home? Who will do what Jesus is asking even if it seems hard?

The answer to these questions in one small way involves me. Several years ago, I met with county representatives in our city to learn what our church could do to help them. During this meeting, I learned that our city had 197 orphans and only fifty homes available to them. They also told me that 50 percent of these children were under the age of five, which I found surprising because I always thought orphans were in the ten- to fifteen-year-old category.

Who will do what Jesus is asking even if it seems hard?

So, I returned home and explained to my wife that I thought our church could help meet this need with some recruiting help. I then told Wendy that I thought our family could also do something to help. She was very excited! She said this was something she had been praying about for years and just was not sure how I would ever come to this decision. She really saw God working on my heart and leading us together into being foster parents in His timing. We had the ability to foster at least one little boy or girl, but I remember feeling resistance as I contemplated the extra time, energy, resources, and space that would be needed for an additional child in our home. Would I need to change a diaper again? Not a fun thought. I wanted to move on with my life and not go back to raising preschoolers again. My children were in grade school and middle school by that time, and life was just getting a little easier. So, I struggled. Finally, though, I listened to the direction I sensed from the Holy Spirit and picked up a foster care application from our local foster care office.

Wendy was thrilled! We came together as a couple and started telling our friends and family about this new step of faith to help serve our community. I was not sure what this would entail but committed to just take it one step at a time.

Soon after, we had our first little girl in our home and cared for her for over eighteen months. I will never forget when I first saw her in the car seat only a few months old. She gave me a big smile, and that was it. She had my heart. Sometimes it's just that easy. We then had the opportunity to adopt her. That was a big decision, but by that point, she was already a part of our family, and the decision made sense in many ways. We knew that her life would be changed forever and that she would have an opportunity to see Jesus lived out in our lives. She would now be able to go to church regularly with us and hear about the Lord. This would provide her with an open door to follow Jesus for herself one day and in so doing be adopted into the kingdom of heaven.

A fascinating observation Wendy and I made was that our family grew more spiritually in those eighteen months of being foster parents than in any other time before it. We were seeking the things of God like never before as a family. We were on a mission together, and it was not about us but about Jesus. Our children embraced the mission of sharing our home, their toys, rooms, and time with someone new. They saw the big picture and loved the difference they were seeing in this little two-year-old girl. The hardest part for me was simply saying *yes* and walking through the doors of foster care, but the greatest reward was also ahead of me. This journey was about exploring what we could do to help save a child in need and in so doing extend God's redemptive plan to others in our world.

But then it happened again. We got another call to foster two more children. That would have been a total of six children in our home and much more work than I had originally bargained for. My wife and I talked it over and agreed to simply foster, with no intention of adopting these additional children. It would be a short-term experience, we thought, and then we would be back to raising our other four children. Both of the new foster children, however, came to the point of needing to be adopted, and the state asked us if we were willing. Would we be the ones to answer this call? Would we take six children into our lives? It seemed like Nineveh for me because it was hard, it seemed long, and it was forever. What would we do? We prayed and prayed. I told God that my answer was going to be *no* unless He made it very clear in the other direction. Then, within twenty-four hours of that prayer, I received seven confirmations affirming that God was with me in this. Some of those confirmations were small, and some were large, but mostly they were prophetic in nature like something we had never seen before. It was clear that God cared about this decision and that these two little lives mattered very much to Jesus.

Then God's confirming hand moved again. He confirmed what He was doing at the end of summer 2016 when we finally decided to move forward with the adoption process of the two additional children. On that day we contacted a man in our church who flipped homes on the side and told us that God had clearly spoken to him. He told us that he was supposed to help us in some way but did not know how or why. He told us simply to call him if we ever needed anything. So, we did. We called and told him we did not have room in our home anymore for this new family size and wanted to get his thoughts about what we could do. He told us that just a few days earlier he had bought a foreclosed home and almost called us six times to see if we would have any interest—but he never called. Then when *we* called *him*, he knew this was our house if we wanted it. He offered to make it happen for us with no additional costs except those associated with the foreclosure. Therefore, we were able to get a home with more space for the foster children at the same price as what our current home cost. It was a pretty amazing opportunity. The problem was that we still had to sell our existing home. Within twenty-four hours, though, we had two offers on our house, accepted one of them, and bought the new house. This was all without even listing our home for sale. It was quite an amazing transaction because without even trying, we had sold our house and God provided another home to meet our needs *on the same day.* God had done it again, confirming that He was on this journey once we submitted and committed to His redemptive plan for creation. Everything else fell into place after that.

God provided another home to meet our needs *on the same day.*

I believe that the way God intervened in our lives through that situation illustrates that adoption, foster care, and helping orphans is not just a good idea but at the heart of the gospel. Caring for orphans becomes a living testimony of God's love and saving work for His people. Even if adopting these children turns out to be the worst decision I ever made, it will still be the best decision I ever made because of its eternal purpose. My life has been changed, my walk with the Lord has been changed, and my family is more missional today because of adoption and foster care than ever before in our lives. It all began with a sense that we could make a difference if we were willing to do something hard for God, and my prayer is that it ends with three little children being liberated from their sins and adopted as children of God.

Below are stories of four more couples who went through a similar journey. May God use their stories to inform, inspire, and encourage you as you look for ways to live out James 1:27.

CHAPTER 2

Scott and Kristie

Written by Pastor Wendy Griffith

Scott and Kristie had always dreamed of having a large family, but after having two healthy baby boys they suffered several heartbreaking losses. While they contemplated international adoption, it was foster care that came to the forefront through various conversations and within the community. Even as they wrestled with their faith during their losses, they knew that God was leading them. They trusted that He would provide and that He knew the desire of their hearts. As God continued to lead them and open doors, they took the next steps to learn more about how foster care might be a part of God's plan for their family. They clung to the Cross in their sorrow, but also in their hope.

Prior to foster care, Scott and Kristie had had some general awareness of poverty, mental health issues, and the judicial system. They had always felt protective and compassionate toward single parents and were aware of housing instability and food insecurities. However, having an awareness and walking that out with biological parents on a daily basis quickly changed their perspective. Biological parents' needs become the needs of their child(ren), and in turn those needs became Scott and Kristie's. This couple danced intimately with undeniable need, true desperation, and significant heartache within their own community. They saw firsthand their community, often neighbors, friends, and family provide resources, love, and support for the parents of their foster children to help get their families reunited. They witnessed programs and agendas that really were helping, and they watched parents receive help with open arms.

The outpouring of love for those less fortunate felt so humbling to Scott and Kristie—as was the conviction of dear friends and family to walk in the suffering and hardship with their foster and adopted children. Their small church came together and did many things to support their fostering journey. Providing Thanksgiving dinners several years, offering clothing or material needs, words of encouragement and praise were remarkable blessings that ministered to this family on their hardest days. One sweet couple on several occasions would take their children for a night or two so they could get away together to recharge. These moments ministered to their marriage and their children at the same time as they watched others come to fostering through *their* family's "yes" to God and decide that they too, could make a difference in the life of a child in need.

They watched others come to fostering through *their* family's "yes" to God.

Scott and Kristie have continued to use their fostering experiences as a way to advocate and grow in social awareness, race relations, special needs parenting, and advocacy. So much good has come from their season as foster parents as well as from the love their 'village' has given to others.

One of the more difficult aspects of foster care has been the long-term commitment fostering takes before coming to resolution. Cases can take a long time, and family healing can take time, causing the child to stay in foster care longer than anticipated. That of course leads to attachment with a child, so naturally, saying goodbye is hard and joyful all at once. Another challenge foster parents have is navigating the occasional tensions with birth families or social workers while simultaneously working hard to be a stabilizing person in the life of a child in need.

One example is to come alongside birth parents during a very difficult time and show them the love of Christ with a smile and encouraging word. Scott and Kristie openly shared the gospel with so many families that they have worked with; they take great pride in the love and attention they provided each child and their biological families. With the knowledge that any one of us could find ourselves in need of intimate support, they always tried their best to never judge a parent's shortcomings. Through the eight years of fostering, they feel so fortunate to still have meaningful relationships with many of their four adopted children's birth parents—even opening their home monthly for dinner with their youngest two children's birth mom, Liz. She has become a part of the family, and they are eternally grateful for her connection to her children post-adoption.

Another one of Scott and Kristie's adopted sons (who they adopted over six years ago) was recently reacquainted with his biological mother due to his younger brother being placed into foster care in Scott and Kristie's home. It was a joy to provide a safe place to their adopted son's half-brother and witness a different outcome—one of reunification! This time the biological mother was successful, and that opportunity has opened many doors for their son to get to know her better in this new season.

Scott and Kristie's entire family has been forever changed by partnering with the needs of others, watching hope ignite with each accomplishment, and seeing a family that was once fractured be restored. The meaningful relationships with each child, their biological families, and the foster care community have created an amazing ripple effect within their own community, church, and family. When one family steps into the brokenness, it has a multiplication effect like no other.

After eight years of fostering and twenty-one placements, the large family Scott and Kristie had always prayed for is now complete with six beautiful children who call them Mom and Dad. All along, God heard the desires of their hearts and prepared them for one of the highest callings.

CHAPTER 3

Michael and Jen

Written by Pastor Wendy Griffith

It is always fun to watch how God connects the dots that seem insignificant or unrelated. In the Spring of 1999, Michael and Jen Dant accepted a position in children's ministry at our home church. We had been filling that role in a volunteer capacity for a few years while finishing our own college educations. We quickly became fast friends; we crammed a lot of laughter, ministry, and fun into the short year and a half they were with us until accepting a new ministry position in Texas. They served faithfully in that role while pursuing their lifelong dream—they felt called to serve children overseas as missionaries. They pursued this calling seriously, but due to extenuating circumstances, they ended up not being able to go on the mission field.

In a season of uncertainty, God was still working even through their disappointments. Years later, I had a specific conversation with Jen. She was walking to pick up her kids from school when I shared my heart and passion and then said, "Jen, I really think it's not *if* you foster, but *when*." At the time, Jen had dozens of excuses for why that was great for others but would not fit into their plan. This conversation was a marked moment for the Dant family because unbeknown to them, a seed began to take root for the new season God had them entering. Adoption was not a foreign concept for either of them. Jen's father passed away tragically when she was just two years old, and she was later adopted by her stepfather at the age of five. Michael, too, had an amazing story of adoption in his own family.

Soon Michael and Jen decided to take the next step and connected with a fantastic child placement agency in their community, Hope and Home. Their philosophy helped to define the Dants' calling, "missional work done right here in our community." Mike and Jen could nurture these children from hard places—right in their very own home. At that time, they really felt that this was a way to fulfill their call to missions.

Mike and Jen felt God changing their perspective. Their heart as a family—to show Jesus's love to kids—had been a central theme in their lives since before they were married and had taken many forms over the years. In the Bible, they had seen the Father's heart toward the most vulnerable and wanted to join Him in that in their own community. Eventually they said *yes* to foster care, and they now see foster care as one of the most impactful ways to show Jesus's love to kids and as a practical, literal way for their family to care for those near and dear to the heart of the Father.

It was incredibly humbling for Mike and Jen to walk through a really challenging time in the life of a child and their family, to show love and care on behalf of the Father, and to realize there are real faces and real stories behind statistics. This had changed everything for them.

One of the biggest challenges for Jen was the lack of control. She felt that loving a child so much, but in the end not having control of the outcome for that child was really hard. To hold the child's future with open hands has felt so difficult. Even so, the goal of foster care is to reunite a child with their first family. Mike and Jen have had the privilege to cheer many parents on and have celebrated their successes! Letting go of the desire to control the process and outcomes is the most challenging aspect. Mike and Jen will never forget watching a little boy drive away from their home in tears as the caseworker had come to move him to a family member's home. Even though they were a safe choice, and they were biological family members, he cried because he just didn't remember them. In that raw moment they wanted to scoop him up and tell him everything would be OK. It can be difficult when the choice you have is to give them a hug, but you need to let them go.

Letting go of the desire to control the process and outcomes is the most challenging aspect.

The biggest highlight of Mike and Jen's fostering journey has been adopting their youngest son. He is the biggest gift that they didn't even know they needed!! God was able to redeem what started out as a tough situation and put His love and grace on display.

They also had the opportunity to celebrate the reunification of two sisters with their parents. The Dants hosted a celebration at their local park with a cake and at the parents' request prayed over their family as the girls returned home that day. While they were focused on providing a loving and nurturing home for these girls, the Father was focusing on the parents and revealing His love, grace, and blessing in their lives. In a rare and sacred moment, two families were brought together by difficult circumstances and able to celebrate the restoration of the family.

Mike and Jen have received various aspects of support from their church community and other friends. Some friends made themselves available around the clock for Mike and Jen to reach out to to pray as a new child was on their way to the Dants' home. Practical help that also came from friends who donated laundry soap, meals, beds, or clothes with little notice has meant everything!

Right after Mike and Jen officially got licensed, they received a call for a placement for two sisters. Over the first few days, they spent time getting to know them and asking for all of their favorites—their favorite color, activities, food. When they got to the favorite food, the youngest sister lit up and said, "*Menudo*!" Jen had to google what that even was, and as it turns out, it is a soup she had never heard of, let alone made. So, she immediately phoned a friend to ask the best place to get this. She told Jen where she could get the ingredients and that she would walk her through making it. Before Jen could get to the store herself, however, this dear friend had not only purchased all of the ingredients, but she made it and brought it over for the girls. It was wonderful to watch these sweet girls realize that not only would they have the love of the Dant family, but also those in their circle of influence would embrace and love them as well. This is where supporting foster families in simple, practical ways encourages them to continue to minister to children in need and keep their doors open.

Supporting foster families in simple, practical ways encourages them to continue to minister to children in need and keep their doors open.

Mike and Jen think that the biggest impact their family has seen is for others to realize that they can make a difference in the lives of kids. Even if they don't directly open their home, they can support families who do. Prayer, meals, laundry soap, *menudo*—all are vital ways of supporting families who foster.

We see a lot of adoption language in Scripture. From the beginning of their journey, Mike and Jen's hearts were open to adoption, but they knew that adoption would come with a mixture of joy and pain. Each story is unique and very personal. Each story continues to be written daily. Mike and Jen feel incredibly honored and blessed to be a part of their youngest son's story and to have grafted him into their family.

The Dants have seen so much life change in the lives of foster kids—and the families of these kids—who have come through their home. They feel that the biggest life change has been their own. Their perspectives, their levels of compassion, and the way they view people all have changed. One of their biggest concerns about opening their home was how it would affect their three biological children. While they have been a part of heartbreak and have seen difficult things, the amount of compassion and empathy that they have for others has grown exponentially! To be a part of life change in others, everything has changed in them as they pressed into what it really means to have the heart of the Father!

CHAPTER 4

John and Alicia

Written by Pastor Wendy Griffith

In life there are people who you immediately know are all the good things that friendship and community offer. The Johnsons are those people. Before we had even moved a single thing into our new home when we transplanted to Kenosha, John and Alicia were there. John helped me paint almost every room, and Alicia was ready to help or answer any questions that a young mom could imagine. They welcomed us into their life group and their home with open arms.

There were a host of factors and experiences that led John and Alicia to foster. Perhaps foremost was foster families they knew who gave them exposure into the fostering community.

It is no surprise to us that John and Alicia journeyed into fostering. It is in their DNA to help and to welcome those who need it most. There were a host of factors and experiences that led John and Alicia Johnson to foster. Perhaps foremost was foster families they knew who gave them exposure into the fostering community. They realized through observing these families that maybe they too could begin to explore foster care. As a teacher, Alicia had always had a passion for children, and they had been involved in children's ministries for many years. John had volunteered with Royal Family Kids Camp, a camp specialized for children in foster care. All of these were steppingstones that slowly aided their decision to begin the fostering journey.

John and Alicia's local church would often highlight the need for foster homes within their southeastern Wisconsin community. The church was operating and supporting several community ministries that support families in need and provided wraparound care for county foster homes. Their passion for children's ministry gave them a heart for kids who needed a safe place to stay with the hope of sharing God's love with them.

James 1:27 is a common verse in the foster community that really resonated with them as a family: "Religion that God our Father accepts as pure and faultless is this: [It's hard to read a verse like this about the heart of God and not feel some conviction] to look after orphans and widows in their distress and to keep oneself from being polluted by the world." The Johnsons knew that there are many different reasons kids end up in foster care, with the root cause overwhelmingly being some sort of breakdown of the family unit.

The Johnsons quickly came to recognize and appreciate that foster parents are a very loving community, which is not always the image you think of based on movie and other cultural references.

One of the greatest realizations for John and Alicia and so many foster parents is that most parents who have lost their kids to foster care still very much love their children. This should underscore just how strong the pull of this world can be, causing some parents to make bad decisions and others to face tragic situations outside their control.

Foster kids are just that—*kids.* They laugh and play, are uniquely brilliant or talented, and often have a big heart for the people around them. They frequently have problems that they are working through, but are not the 'problem' we often think about when we think of foster kids.

People often say they could never foster, because it would be too hard to love a child and then have to say goodbye. Yes, all of that, but John and Alicia were overwhelmed at the hope and redemption still felt in those difficult moments.

Fostering provides a front row seat to phone calls or sitting in courtrooms with bio-parents completely heartbroken that they can no longer continue parenting. Despite the troubles that separated them, those parents still very much love their kids, and their kids very much love their parents. Watching those relationships break down or become unviable is gut wrenching. Ultimately, watching a child grapple with their place in this world, and hearing them process "Why me?" or "What did I do?" or "Do I matter to my mom or dad or to anyone?"—that is what really challenges the Johnsons. This is where they shine as foster parents as they communicate God's love and hope in every situation.

Children in foster care can have many issues to work through but most often are very sweet kids. Most of their older foster kids have called them "Mom" and "Dad" because that is what they are to them for that season of their life. Today, they are currently fostering a one-and-a-half-year-old who they describe as 100,000% adorable and makes their family all smile as he discovers the world around him.

In the past eight years and counting the Johnson family has provided a haven for over twelve placements and multiple short-term respite placements. As a result of John and Alicia's *yes*, neighbors on either side of them have started fostering in part from hearing and seeing their story. They also have been so blessed to step back into the lives of former foster children in ways they thought they would no longer experience as parents because the child had been placed elsewhere or had been reunified with their parents.

John and Alicia's heart was to provide a safe place for a child until they could be reunited with their family, so they did not originally sign up to foster as an adoptive resource. However, they have since adopted a beautiful teen girl! She was one of their first placements and with them for over four years in foster care. They watched option after option fall through for her. She had parents and extended family who loved her but could not turn a corner to bring her back into their family. John and Alicia are still in regular contact with many of them, which in some ways is beautiful and in other ways complicated. There will likely always be some tension over the "What ifs" and "What could have beens," but their adopted daughter knows that she is loved by an amazing family and many others; she knows that John and Alicia will always be in her corner to cheer her on.

God compares His relationship to us as a husband to His bride, and as a Father to His children—adopted into His family. John and Alicia believe that while their heart is not as noble as God's, they value and appreciate the Father's love for them in a greater capacity after being foster and adoptive parents.

CHAPTER 5

Gary and Patty

Written by Pastor Wendy Griffith

Gary and Patty Miller were in their thirties when they got married and started planning for a family. After seven discouraging years, their greatest miracle, Garrett, arrived, and just two years after him their sweet baby girl, Grace. They thought their family was complete and that God had answered their prayers. Life appeared perfect—until it wasn't. Less than two years after Grace's arrival, their son Garrett became very sick and was diagnosed with leukemia. Eight short months later, surrounded by his family, Garrett went to be with Jesus. Their whole world was turned upside-down, and the consequences and fallout from that would change everything. Both Patty and Gary struggled to maintain hope in their devastation, but their two-year-old daughter needed them now more than ever. They would tell you that this period was the darkest time in their lives and marriage, but even then, God was making a way.

When Grace was four years old, they began looking into foster care to help distract from their own grief and provide a sibling experience for their daughter as they all navigated this new season without their beloved son and brother. Patty and Gary believed that God could use their own brokenness and loss to help another family and as a result be encouraged that their family still had purpose and hope. When they first began their fostering journey, they did not know of any families fostering in the community. As a result of their *yes*, years later our own family's story in fostering began. The Millers were a catalyst of a movement that God was birthing in our community, church, and family.

Welcoming a stranger into their home was the distraction Gary and Patty needed most. The realization that children were facing difficulties and heartache with little understanding as to the why was heartbreaking for them. One *yes* and one child at a time, the Millers found their way and started pouring love into the hearts of so many in their community who needed them to show up each day. The cloud of grief was being lifted one story at a time for the children and for their own family.

The Millers were a catalyst of a movement that God was birthing in our community, church, and family.

During this season there were several opportunities to adopt children—opportunities that for one reason or another fell through. One day those *nos* became a *yes* when they welcomed little Delicia Delray into their home. She was seven months old and stole their hearts from the first hello. A year and a half later, she was an official Miller. She was worth the wait, and yet God had more for this dedicated family. At the time of Delicia's adoption, two young brothers came for a respite visit. Shortly after, they ended up placed in the Millers' home, and their journey to become official members of the family began. God knew that even in their moment of deep grief that Patty and Gary would have a reason to celebrate all that God had done in and through them. Mateo and Aidan were what they had been waiting for. Their family was complete! During over sixteen years of fostering, the Millers had shared their home with over seventeen children and provided countless respite opportunities for other fostering families.

When Patty and Gary decided that their season of fostering was closing, they began to look for new ways to still make a difference in the growing foster care community. One realization was that over the sixteen years they had fostered, the support or lack thereof within the community significantly impacted longevity of fostering families. They were committed to the process of being that support for other families on their journey to help hurting children. The wraparound support they provided so many was integral in many families' success and in several children returning or finding their forever home.

The Millers are just one example of many families who entered foster care with their own brokenness and then watched God work miracle after miracle in their own family and hearts! These two people committed to God made a way in the wilderness even when they could not see it. Because of that, countless lives have been impacted and changed forever.

PART TWO

The Biblical Mandate

Several passages of Scripture support and more clearly define the issue of adoption and foster care from a theological perspective. Part Two provides a brief biblical-theological overview of themes such as compassion, rescue, and adoption with respect to caring for the most vulnerable among us—children. This theme of caring for the vulnerable also can be seen throughout the Torah and the Psalms:[1]

- Warning not to mistreat any fatherless child (Exod 22:22).
- God requires Israel to be on guard and speaks of a curse to come on anyone who tries to hurt those in need of justice (Deut 24:17; 27:19).
- Agricultural leaders were required to leave produce in fields for the hungry (Deut 24:19-21).
- Every third year, the marketplace would give a tithe to the poor (Deut 26:12-13).
- God is the Father to the fatherless (Ps 68:5).
- God requires justice for the fatherless (Ps 82:3).

God's heart for rescuing the weak can be seen in Deuteronomy when the people of Israel are delivered from slavery, and the love God has for them is demonstrated by freeing them from a life of bondage. Israel was on a journey through the wilderness to redemption in the Promised Land.[2] The nation of Israel teaches us much about our journey as we read about theirs. Additionally, the instructions from God as He interacted with the Israelites inform us on how we should live and respond to Christ today.[3] For example, as Achtemeier says, "In Deuteronomy 7:6-11, Israel was chosen as God's people. Not because they were the strongest or the greatest nation. She was a nation of a mixed multitude, not wise, not powerful and not noble at birth. However, that the world would see them released from Egypt was by God's hand and not theirs."[4] God chose to save a people that needed saving and demonstrated His love and His power at the same time.

To delve more specifically into the theology of care for the vulnerable (including orphans), chapters 2-5 in Part Two of this book examine passages from Isaiah, Acts, James, and Romans both to see God's heart of compassion and how the Church—having itself received the spirit of adoption into God's family and empowered by the Spirit, can and must demonstrate that spirit of adoption in the lives of others to care for them. These passages demonstrate God's heart for those needing rescue, answer the question of why the church should prioritize ministry to vulnerable children, and how caring for these children is at the heart of the gospel.

Isaiah begins the conversation with a strong word for God's people in the Old Testament, and that mandate continues into the New Testament. These passages also show how this message carries forward to the first-century Church and to every Christ follower in the future through the words of James and Paul. Paul's theology of adoption is key to informing the basis for Christian efforts in the modern-day foster care movement and a beautiful vision for how the love of God redesigns us all.

CHAPTER 6

Compassion for Orphans

The concept of compassion flows throughout Scripture and is an essential part of how Christians respond to orphans in their community. "Compassion will help you be tolerant of a child's deep neediness, and to be forgiving when he or she does not understand something that seems so basic, like how to sit at a dining room table with the family, how to use toilet paper, or how to read facial expressions."[1] Jesus had compassion on the marginalized of His time. He also has compassion for us today. It is compassion that allows us to understand what others have been through and empathize with others to the point of getting involved. True compassion does not just sit on the couch and feel bad for someone, but rather jumps into action to helps someone in need. Karyn Purvis, David Cross, and Wendy Sunshine put it this way when speaking about neglected children:

> The lives that many of them have endured were more difficult than we [could] fathom. With compassion, a parent can look inside their child's heart and recognize the impairments and deep fears that drive maladaptive behavior—fears of abandonment, hunger, being in an

> unfamiliar environment, losing control, and being hurt.[2]

It is this compassion that moves our expectations to a realistic level. We can express the fruit of the Spirit when caring for children who do not trust adults or who have never had healthy attachment before. It is compassion that demonstrates love and compels us to be joyful and celebrate the moments when a child does the smallest thing right. Compassion puts others first and our concerns second. It is compassion that spurs us on to be faithful when we feel like giving up or being kind when a child yells at us in frustration. "Deep down, these children want desperately to connect and succeed but don't understand how. As parents, it is our job to show them."[3] Compassion, as Purvis, Cross, and Sunshine call it, is our touchstone.[4] It is love, and love is the thesis of God's Word.

Compassion identifies and cares for those who have literally or metaphorically been beaten up, stripped, and left for dead, as the traveler in the parable of the Good Samaritan (Luke 10:25-37).

Compassion identifies and cares for those who have literally or metaphorically been beaten up, stripped, and left for dead, as the traveler in the parable of the Good Samaritan (Luke 10:25–37). It encourages Christ-followers to extend God's grace by helping tangibly. Compassion is not merely feeling sad for those in need; it is acting with love and provision. The Scriptures call us to clothe ourselves with compassion, because the need cries out for more than just emotional attachment[5] (Col 3:12).

Children are a blessing from the Lord, and Christ followers are encouraged to be intentional in protecting children from foolishness, rebellion, and a life of sin (Prov 22:6). With the help of a loving church family, children can lead healthy, long, protected lives[6] (Exod

20:12). The need and the call reach far beyond our biological children and into the lives of the most vulnerable among us.

God's compassionate nature is seen throughout Scripture, as has been seen in Scriptures from the Torah and the Psalms. The Prophet Isaiah includes orphans as people who need compassion.

Isaiah 1:17

"Learn to do good; seek justice; correct oppression; bring justice to the fatherless and plead the widow's cause" (Isa 1:17, ESV). The New Living Translation states it even more plainly: "Learn to do good. Seek justice. Help the oppressed. Defend the cause of orphans. Fight for the rights of widows" (Isa 1:17, NLT).

There is much to learn from this passage of Scripture as it illuminates the character of God and further describes what it means to serve Him.

- This verse clarifies the significance of this issue to the heart of God and makes a connection between orphan care and the Christian life.
- In this verse, God brings marginalized people to the front lines of the spiritual battle. He connects the way a nation cares for the orphan with the degree to which God's people truly know who God is. Only people that love the widows and the orphans know the heart of God.
- This passage commands followers of God to examine their worship and stop doing rituals meant to gain favor with God but instead help the marginalized in the community. It is those acts of worship that reveal an accurate understanding of God's heart and represent who He is to the world in need.

God wants His people to help the orphans and widows. To overlook the fatherless is to overlook the gospel because God shows His love by rescuing those who have no provider. Put another way, the church can do many things, but if it overlooks the orphan, it overlooks God.

The modern world has not escaped the need to care for orphans as illustrated by the over 400,000 children without a parent to care for them in the U.S. alone.[7] This segment of the population is at high risk of incarceration and human trafficking after high school if a permanent home is not identified.[8] Therefore, since the need for orphan care is still real today, who should be addressing it? Should it be government programs, private group homes, or medical facilities designed to address this population? What about Christians?

Does Isaiah 1:17 imply that *every* Christian should be involved? The following chapter begins by exploring Isaiah 1:17 as it relates to caring for orphans. It seeks to understand how important this issue is to our relationship with God and explores the connection between orphan care and the Christian life, using Isaiah 1:17 to gain perspective.

There is much to learn from this passage of Scripture as it illuminates the character of God and further describes what it means to serve him. The Book of Isaiah is significant because it sets the tone for themes of prophecy that are repeated in Jeremiah and Ezekiel.[9] Isaiah 1 is a review of the literary, historical, and theological scope of the whole book.[10] The prophet Isaiah and God go into detail and exercise great patience with the people of Israel as they call out sin and ask the people to turn back to God.[11]

The evidence that a person knows God is found in their ethical behavior toward the oppressed.

Isaiah presents two pathways for the nation of Israel: the wrong way that will lead to separation from God and the right way that leads to blessing. Interestingly, the right way is described in chapter 1:16-17.[12] The Israelites think that as long as they participate in offerings to God that they are entitled to His favor. They learn, however, from the prophet Isaiah, that the person who acts like God knows Him—not merely someone who makes offerings to Him.[13] The evidence that a person knows God is found in their ethical behavior toward the oppressed.[14]

At this time in history, religious symbols represented the condition of the heart; therefore, if the heart of the people was not aligned with what mattered to God, their offerings of worship meant nothing.[15] Karl N. Jacobson points out that "Isaiah is more than simply prophesying or predicting, it is deep in teaching, warnings, and encouragement."[16] Isaiah 1:17 calls Israel to radical repentance.[17] There is a sense of urgency in the first chapter of Isaiah to warn the people of their separation from God and the impending disaster to come if they do not repent. Isaiah says that the Israelites have been reduced to a level even lower than animal status because "The ox knows its master"[18] (Isa 1:3, NIV). In other words, the way they were behaving indicated they no longer knew the Lord.

The Lord is a God of justice, and because justice is the character of God, the Prophet Isaiah strongly calls the nation of Israel to be a just nation.[19] The idea of justice is exemplified by how a culture decides human relationships should exist between members of the community and therefore is a social concept.[20] Since justice is a social concept, it is helpful to understand that Israel was a kinship society that placed a focus on ancestral and generational structures. As a result, the extended family was assigned the role of rescuing a member of the family if they fell into debt, lost a husband, or were forced into slavery.[21] Sojourners, widows, and orphans did not have a family unit to care for them and as a result were the most vulnerable of society. Orphans had no parents alive to care for them, and a widow had no husband to care for her, having married into a home where her husband had died, from sickness or from battle.[22]

Susan Niditch contends that the structure of Isaiah 1:4-20 is that of a sermon because of the style, tone, and way in which the speaker addresses the audience.[23] She makes the point that Isaiah uses these verses to preach like a poet would use a poem.[24] As in many sermons, a strong warning is issued in Isaiah 1:2-20. The people of Israel were warned and then compared to Sodom and Gomorrah because of their disobedience and lack of justice.[25]

God could have told them to do many things that were just, but He chose care for widows and orphans as the focus of His compassion because it is His nature to rescue those lost and in need of saving.

Isaiah 1:17 is located in a book of the Bible written to warn and guide God's people back to Him. Isaiah was the prophet assigned by God to tell the people of their wrong and wicked ways in hopes that they would avoid disaster and return to a life of blessing and protection. Chapter 1 of Isaiah spends the first fifteen verses explaining wrong ways of living and what will happen if the Israelites do not turn back to God. Verse 16 tells the people to stop doing what they are doing, and only one verse tells the people what they should do instead—verse 17. God could have told them to do many things that were just, but He chose care for widows and orphans as the focus of His compassion because it is His nature to rescue those lost and in need of saving.

The tone used in verse 17 is mostly that of command and imperative producing a strong suggestion that a change in behavior will lead to a better tomorrow. The encouraging tense is hard to grasp in a straightforward reading of the text because of the strong command tone, but it is precisely that sense of encouragement that gives the verse its power and vision for the future.

The New Testament echoes the teachings of Isaiah and describes the empowerment available to the church to help the marginalized in the Book of Acts, as seen in the section below.

CHAPTER 7

Empowerment to Care for Orphans

Backdrop of the Gospels

The Gospels of Matthew, Mark, Luke, and John talk about the life of Christ in a way that describes Him as a seed that has died for our sins and has been placed in the ground. Christ then was raised from the grave, and the next chapter of human history began. The Book of Acts describes the fruit that is then produced from this spectacular part of the story (John 12:24). We see Jesus going first to the Jews, then to the Gentiles, and eventually producing a movement that influenced Rome.[1]

Acts is called the Acts of the Apostles and describes in the first chapter the commissioning of the disciples to be witnesses of what Christ had done for them (Acts 1:8). Then, the following chapters outline an account of the Holy Spirit empowering people to witness about Christ. During this time, the Early Church expanded and showed God's love to many new parts of the world.[2]

Luke was a traveler and often writes in his Gospel about places he visited. For example, he writes about Mary and Joseph and the inn (Luke 2:7). He also writes about the Samaritan who helped the wounded Jew at an inn (Luke 10:34–35). In Acts, Luke clearly explains Paul's travels including details such as the last small island. Luke writes about how Jesus ate with people and told parables with them over dinner. He does this more than any other writer. Luke also has a strong concern for the oppressed and the poor. He notes unfair treatment of people groups like the Samaritans and eunuchs. He also points out people with limited opportunities and privileges. Luke is outspoken about the rich and their failure to help those in need when the need was clearly in front of them.[3]

In Luke's time, socioeconomic class divisions existed, and slavery was normal. Approximately two percent of the population was wealthy, and half of the people lived at or below the poverty level for portions of their lives.[4] As a doctor, no doubt he was aware of the suffering and injustices around him. The story he recounts in Acts 6—discussed below—has strongly impacted the mission of Christ to those who are poor and has set an example for church leaders today. It sheds light on how the Early Church practically handled the tension of meeting needs and serving others with unity, seeking to understand more about the role of serving the poor as the body of Christ. In this chapter, we see that not only does God mandate care for the marginalized, but He also empowers His people through the Spirit to do just that.

Acts: Empowerment to Respond to and Care for the Marginalized

The local church began in the Book of Acts, and in this book, we find in chapter 6 lay leaders given the authority to carry out the work of helping the widows and the orphans who were hungry. The Bible says when speaking of the chosen volunteers, "These seven were presented to the apostles, who prayed for them as they laid their hands on them" (NLT). At this point the volunteer leaders took on this new task with the blessing of leadership. The fact that the apostles laid hands on them and prayed showed value in them and demonstrated that the work they were about to do with the widows was godly and spiritual work. These church leaders could have appointed the new men into service and moved on with their work, but instead, they chose to commission them through prayer. This simple yet necessary step demonstrated the apostles' trust in this new team and validated the importance of the lay leader's work to the kingdom of God. It added value to the newly appointed team in the eyes of the Hebrew and Greek people moving forward.

The mantle of leadership needed to be passed on by the leaders themselves for the people to respect the new structure. The new leadership team had a passion that continued even after their commissioning, and they witnessed for Christ like never before. This newly delegated authority did not weaken the ministry or the spiritual impact of the ministry in any way; it simply multiplied it.[5]

In the same way, the church of today can model this action by selecting volunteers who God will bless as they lead the effort of caring for foster children in the community. Acts 2:45 is another place the Early Church took action to help those in need. Christ followers helped the Christians around the table and all the people in their community that were in need. Their sacrificial actions of selling possessions and helping the poor set the tone for future generations to follow.

The importance of this passage can be seen in how the church today struggles to meet the overwhelming needs of the community through volunteer service using limited resources. The pressure is high for the twenty-first-century church, yet the first-century church sets an example applicable for today.

Acts 6 has the potential to motivate Christians today because, as more understanding is gained about how Christ wants believers to live, the possibility for empowered living becomes far greater. Acts 6:1-7 provides a vivid example of how the Early Church empowered people to serve the poor with generosity and loving relationships.

> As the believers rapidly multiplied, there were rumblings of discontent. The Greek-speaking

> believers complained about the Hebrew-speaking believers, saying that their widows were being discriminated against in the daily distribution of food (Acts 6:1, NLT).

The Early Church was not very organized and did not have the structure, buildings, and systems it has today. The government of the church was strongly democratic, and people gave voluntarily to help the poor. Eventually, people got jobs and provided for themselves, but the widows were unable to work. They were a people group left behind and in need.[6]

There was a conflict that arose in the body of Christ between the Greek-speaking Jews and the Hebraic Jews. This conflict was centered around the widows of each culture within the newly formed Christian Church because they were not receiving the same type of care that should have been given to all. The idea of overlooking the widows because of cultural differences was a huge problem for the Jerusalem church, and this was a critical moment for the leadership to decide how they would address it. Conflict can be used for good, unifying groups and helping them to find common ground. It can also be used for harm and division within families, organizations, and the church. In this case, the disciples were faced with a decision about how to equally and fairly take care of the widows in both cultures. The way they handled this problem had a long-lasting impact on the future of the church because at this point it was growing in number, influence, and resources. The impact the church was having could continue to grow or be set back depending on how this situation was handled. The following is a breakdown of the scriptures around Acts 6:6 intended to explore the actions of the disciples from an exegetical point of view.

Acts 6:2

"So, the Twelve called a meeting of all the believers. They said we apostles should spend our time teaching the word of God, not running a food program" (Acts 6:2, NLT).

The disciples responded to the tension of the situation by reminding the people of their primary task. They were called to preach the word and pray. This was their gifting, and they did not want to get off task for other good and necessary things that needed to be done. So, the disciples started with purpose and reminded the people of what their purpose was in the big picture. They did not focus on the complaining attitude toward leadership and become defensive. There was a real problem, and they wanted to see it fixed. They called a meeting with the people and started by stating the vision to remind the people what the Apostles role was in the church. It is worth noting that, when faced with a crisis, the first leaders of the church led with vision. They did not dismiss the importance of caring for the poor but sought a solution that would free them to do what God had called them to do while still helping those in need. The apostles listened to the people and began problem-solving as is seen in the following verse.[7]

Acts 6:3

"And so, brothers, select seven men who are well respected and are full of the Spirit and wisdom. We will give them this responsibility" (Acts 6:3, NLT).

The disciples did not look down on the widows but instead took the matter very seriously. They formed the first volunteer leadership team in the church and delegated responsibility to them. These leaders were not asked to preach or be professional speakers but instead to be servants. As leaders, they were asked to serve in practical ministry to widows, and seven men were selected, most likely consistent with the Jewish practice of setting up boards for specific duties. There were three qualifications for these men, but we do not know how they were selected. The qualifications were similar to those in 1 Timothy 3:8-13. Once selected, the disciples turned the work over to them. This implies full empowerment so that they were released to take ownership of the ministry and make decisions.[8]

Acts 6:4

"Then we apostles can spend our time in prayer and teach the word" (Acts 6:4, NLT).

The purpose was again put before the people so that they knew why this decision was being made. It is evident in this verse that the heart of the Apostles was to keep the mission clear and the task on course. They did not want to sacrifice the role they had been given. It is also clear that the tension behind this conflict was significant, requiring the stating and restating of why this decision was made. This was not being done because they did not care or did not want to help the widows themselves but because it would pull them away from their primary purposes. They were not saying that they were better than others because they preached, and others should do less critical work, but instead they were restating their primary calling and the desire to stay true to it. Paul describes his ministry in Acts 20:34-35 as doing other things than merely preaching and praying. The disciples served others in a variety of ways but chose this situation to reorganize and create a new structure to care for the growing needs.[9]

Acts 6:5

"Everyone liked this idea, and they chose the following: Stephen (a man full of faith and the Holy Spirit), Philip, Procorus, Nicanor, Timon, Parmenas, and Nicolas of Antioch (an earlier convert to the Jewish faith)" (Acts 6:5, NLT).

All seven of these men seem to be Hellenists. The prevailing thought is that it was wise for them to choose men that were from the culture that was feeling overlooked. In doing so, these new leaders were able to connect best with the culture they were asked to minister to. It also seemed to show respect for the Greek Speaking Jews and in so doing addressed the felt disrespect that was causing the tension to begin with. The overall result was that both sides agreed to the decision and unity prevailed. What was once a point of confusion and possible division had become a unanimous point of unity.

Acts 6:6

"These seven were presented to the apostles, who prayed for them as they laid their hands on them" (Acts 6:6, NLT).

At this point the new volunteer leaders were commissioned for a specific task. The fact that the apostles laid hands on them and prayed showed a value in them and demonstrated that the work they were about to do with the widows was godly and spiritual work. These church leaders could have appointed the new men into service and moved on with their work, but instead, they chose to commission them through prayer. This simple yet necessary step demonstrated their trust in this new team and validated the importance of their work to the kingdom of God. It added value to the newly appointed team in the eyes of the people moving forward.

The mantle of leadership needs to be passed on by the leaders themselves for the people to respect the new structure. It was true then, and that principle remains true today. The new leadership team had a passion that continued even after their commissioning, and they witnessed for Christ like never before. This newly delegated authority did not weaken the ministry or the spiritual impact of the ministry in any way. It simply multiplied it.[10]

Acts 6:7

"So, God's message continued to spread. The number of believers greatly increased in Jerusalem, and many of the Jewish priests were converted, too" (Acts 6:7, NLT).

This verse seems to say that God blessed this decision, and

fruitful ministry was the result. The fact that the church was very multicultural at this time was the source of the tension but also its greatest strength. It could reach more significant numbers of people because of its diversity, and now that this conflict had been successfully settled, unity fueled the growth of the church. Also unusual about this verse is the inclusion of the priests who were converting as well. Most of the priest were Sadducees and did not believe in the resurrection, so this fact was a breakthrough for the growth of the church. This conversion of the priests meant that the gospel had now reached every segment of Jerusalem society.[11] The role of the Spirit can be seen in the wisdom of the Apostles' decision to appoint these seven men full of the Spirit and set them free to accomplish the work of Christ. This evidence of the Spirit's empowerment to organize the church further multiplied the people and set off a new wave of growth.[12] The Greek word *euxanon* was used in this verse and means "was increasing" and "kept growing."[13]

Lessons from Acts about Serving the Poor, Widows, and Orphans

These seven passages of Scripture are presented in narrative form and as such tell a compelling story of the Spirit's work in the Early Church. It is interesting to see how the storyline of the Spirit follows the apostles and then at this juncture changes direction. It seems as though the story begins to follow those, such as Stephen and Phillip, doing the work of helping the widows. They were empowered by the Holy Spirit to be witnesses for Christ and ultimately died for that cause. However, even the death of Stephen was critical for the scattering of the saints and the continued spread of the gospel. Many others in the body of Christ began preaching the gospel other than the apostles, and there may be something to be said for the Spirit's storyline here. Organizing volunteer Christ followers to more effectively serve the vulnerable people in society was consistent with what Jesus asked His people to do before He left the earth. Serving others, therefore, is an activity close to the heart of God because it is the first step in spreading the gospel. God will bless our acts of serving the community in the same way today as He did in the Book of Acts.

Moreover, this exploration of Scripture is the validation of the Pentecostal event earlier in Acts 2:4. The disciples were filled with the power of the Holy Spirit to witness about Christ. They were average people given supernatural power and gifts to advance the mission of Christ. The promise at Pentecost was for every believer, every member of the family, and every class of citizen. It was an event that brought equality to all people to share the gospel. Therefore, we see the seven men selected to lead the ministry to widows as a continuation of this new move of God's Spirit. Average people—believers in Christ—were filled with the Spirit and empowered to carry out the vital work of the church as volunteers. This example brings hope and excitement to the modern church today because volunteers can expect the same possibilities, calling, and results from the power of the Holy Spirit.

Another application of this text has to do with the poor and marginalized because of the direction of the storyline. Once the decision was made to empower volunteers into serving, the storyline of the Spirit follows those that were serving the poor as Christ had asked the church to do. When Christ was on earth, He told the disciples to serve others, and He demonstrated this with his life. Christ began his ministry to the poor in Galilee and taught about the hope found in Him for those who had no hope. His message hit home with this group because at that time there were really only two classes of people, the rich and the poor.

Jesus himself declared that He was the fulfillment of the Isaiah 61 prophecies and therefore had come to set the captives free. It was His stated purpose from the beginning and therefore is in alignment with the powerful move of the Spirit we see in the verses following this decision to minister to the poor. Therefore, it is apparent that ministries to widows, children, and the marginalized are at the very heart of the gospel.

Organizing volunteer Christ followers to more effectively serve the vulnerable people in society was consistent with what Jesus asked His people to do before He left the earth.

External evidence supporting this claim can be found in *The Apologetics Study Bible: Real Questions, Straight Forward Answers, Stronger Faith* where Ted Cabal writes, "The book of Acts stands at the heart of the New Testament."[14] The link is the fact that Luke wrote more about the rich and poor than any other writer and highlighted this purpose as central to the work of Jesus and the disciples. Therefore, if Luke focused on the mission of Christ to set the captives free through the power of the Holy Spirit, and his writings were at the heart of the New Testament describing the New Covenant, then it is reasonable to see a theology of the marginalized as central to the message of the gospel.

The Bible Guide points out that the Jews were used to caring for the orphans and widows together. They fed the orphans with two meals a day as well as caring for the widows with weekly baskets and daily trays of food.[15] As a result, of the Spirit's move through this new team of volunteer leaders the church grew. Many of the priests even began to follow Christ because they saw the church helping the poor and caring for people in need.

It can be concluded, therefore, that serving the poor widows was critical to living out an authentic faith and winning over hearts to Christ. God's blessing was there, and the results were beyond anyone's imagination. This text demonstrates the wisdom of empowering Godly volunteers with the work of the church and the blessing of God on the ministry to the poor. It is a beautiful picture of what the church can look like today.

Acts 9 further emphasizes God's heart for the marginalized as well as the empowerment of the Spirit to serve them. "In Joppa, there was a believer named Tabitha. Her name in the Greek language was Dorcas. She was always doing good and helping poor people" (Acts 9:36, NIRV). Tabitha was an example of a believer who helped the poor and was loved by widows. When she died, many widows specifically gathered around her and were weeping. Her excellent deeds had blessed them over time. This Scripture points out that she was "always doing good" and through her acts of love to the marginalized, she gained favor, trust, and love in return. As Samantha Brewer notes,

> The majority of the first-century Palestinian world was made up of two people groups: the rich and the poor. The religious and socially wealthy could also be categorized into two main groups: the observant Jewish leaders and those associated with the Herodians and Romans who were accepted for their power but made outcasts for their lack of morality.[16]

It is particularly interesting that Luke is writing to his generation as well as to future generations about the importance of following Christ, and as he does, he writes more about the rich and poor than any other writer in the New Testament. It is equally interesting that at the time of Luke (approximately A.D. 80-90) there were only two classes: the rich and the poor. This speaks to Luke's theology of the poor and how vital it was for people to understand how Jesus viewed them. The writings of Luke were being read by predominantly poor and marginalized people. This theology of Christ that gives hope to the poor is precisely what was needed to connect with the people of that day as well as the people of future generations. There is a message of hope and a message of unity to all socioeconomic classes.

Since Luke is the author of both Acts and the Gospel of Luke, it is worth noting that he spends a considerable amount of time teaching about the poor before he gets to Acts. For example, in Luke 5:30-31

Jesus answers them, "Those who are healthy don't need a doctor, sick people do. I have not come to get those who think they are right with God to follow me. I have come to get sinners to turn away from their sins" (Mark 2:17, NIRV).

Serving, generosity, and relationship building are part of caring for a child and increase the opportunity for discipleship.

Other times in Luke we see teaching that leads us to live a life with compassion toward the poor. This can be seen in the Beatitudes (Luke 6:20-26), the story of the Good Samaritan (10:25-27), and the rich young ruler (18:18-23). Dario Lopez Rodriguez in his book *The Liberating Mission of Jesus* points out that there is a recommended path to reaching people for Christ seen in the book of Luke:

> First, we should look at the story of the Good Samaritan as an example of the heart needed to serve others and in so doing gain their trust. Serving others and caring for them even if they are different demonstrates the type of Love Jesus preached about.
>
> The second step is generosity. This was seen in the Good Samaritan story as well. Generosity is a part of serving or may happen directly after someone is helped. This demonstrates love differently. It is one thing to give time to help someone, and it is another to give of your resources. That is a one-two punch to open their heart.
>
> Third is the relational step of befriending sinners: talking to them, accepting them for who they are, and getting to the point where they will call us friends. This culminates with an opportunity at some point to

> share the good news of God's love and forgiveness to them because their heart is open to listening.[17]

All three of these steps can be seen in the foster care process. Serving, generosity, and relationship building are part of caring for a child and increase the opportunity for discipleship. Furthermore, the depth of relationship that can be developed between a parent and child offers incredible opportunity for evangelism that is difficult to achieve through less committed relationships.

CHAPTER 8

Equity for the Poor

To further develop a biblical theology of care for the poor, widows, and orphans as a foundation for Christian commitment to serve in foster care and adoption, I now look to the Book of James, which emphasizes the equity of the poor.[1] The context of James reveals his belief that the outward actions of our lives demonstrate the reality of our faith. James 5:1–6 speaks of not only the condition of the heart that does not care for the poor but also the compounding effect that selfish living by the rich continues to have on those under them economically.[2]

James' teachings, however, connect a variety of topics together that include humility, liberty, self-control, and poverty.[3] Helping the poor, then, becomes an outward result of a holistic life well lived for Christ. It is not possible to separate service to the poor from the authentic Christian life.

James lived in a patriarchal system where the loss of a father meant that a child was an orphan even if the mother was still alive. Therefore, with no man alive to care for the child or the mother, they were the most vulnerable in society.[4] We are reminded further by James that it is only God's perspective that matters in life, and that perspective includes a deep concern for the poor. As long as there is an economic disparity, there will always be a need to love others as ourselves.[5] Therefore, when a need is identified, James believes that it is essential to be quick to act. Words of empathy are not enough for James because people in need require real, practical, and rapid help.[6]

James understood the oppression and pain of those without a parent. He had led the Early Church as it dealt with serving widows and orphans (Acts 6). Then, God through the Apostle James's pen reminds the church to continue to respond in like manner, clarifying that "religion that is pure and undefiled before God, the Father, is this: to visit the orphans and widows in their affliction, and to keep oneself unstained from the world."[12] This verse tells the church that it needs to help widows and orphans but is not specific about *how*. Therefore, while the methodology remains flexible, the mandate to care for orphans is sharp and clear. The church of every generation has the responsibility to determine how it will answer this call.

It is not possible to separate service to the poor from the authentic Christian life.

The second half of James 1:27, to keeping oneself "unstained from the world," is crucial to the point James in making because helping the poor without a life of purity to God does not bring glory to Him. It speaks to our identity with Christ, because any group of people claiming to love the Lord Jesus must understand that He sees us as functional parts of His plan to help the poor.[7] It is part of our identity as Christ followers. Loving the world is a mindset that is opposite of God's heart and feeds the desire for wealth, luxury, envy, and selfish ambition. The church is called to "return to its prophetic role as the outworkers of God's vision of feeding the poor, housing the homeless, visiting the sick, and clothing the naked."[8] What makes a Christian community like the Church authentic in its claims is when a definition like James 1:27 is lived out to the world because faith and then practice send the message of love.[9]

CHAPTER 9

The Spirit of Adoption

A Pneumatology of Foster Care and Adoption

The definition of a prophet is someone who brings an alternative narrative to the dominant Influence of the culture.[1] Foster and adoptive parents are prophetic when they open their home to a child they do not know from the community. The dominant philosophy of culture is to gain privacy, personal wealth, and freedom. The more comfortable that life is, the more successful a person is perceived to be. Therefore, in many ways, foster care and adoption threaten that possibility because they cost extra time, money, and emotional energy. The Spirit, therefore, can be seen moving in the lives of parents as they become tangible, living examples of the gospel through foster care and adoption. This offers the world another way to live in alignment with the heart of the Father, Son, and Holy Spirit.

Pentecostal theology stems from the first half of Acts 2 where the disciples are filled with and empowered by the Holy Spirit for evangelism. It is important to note, however, that the second part of Acts 2 shows what this group of empowered Christ followers *did* with their passion for Christ. They *served and gave* to those in need to demonstrate the love of Christ. Verse 45 says, "They sold property and possessions to give to anyone who had a need" Acts 2:45 (NIV). The Holy Spirit empowers us to care for each other. Today, a passionate approach to helping those in need is to demonstrate God's love in the same way. This aligns with what it means to be led by the Spirit of God, as first demonstrated in Acts 2 where we see compassion as an immediate response to the empowerment of the Holy Spirit. Today, God calls the church once again to make bold decisions with our possessions, ministries, and lives to help the most vulnerable in our communities.

The Holy Spirit empowers us to care for each other.

A follower of Christ sees the gifts of the Spirit operating in harmony with the fruit of the Spirit. When the two operate together, there is power and witness to Christ. Children without a safe home need to see the fruit of the Spirit displayed and encounter the Spirit of God through the believer for themselves. They can see and touch Christ in us as we walk in the Spirit with them every day they are in our homes.

Many abused children have never seen a man be patient or kind. They have never experienced someone speaking a positive prophetic word over his or her life, seen someone healed, or had a reason to be drawn closer to Christ, until they have come into a relationship with a believer in Christ. This is like how, in Exodus 28:31-35, Aaron wore bells with pomegranate fruit in-between to soften the sound and draw the people closer to the Temple to listen more intently. The connection here is that the fruit and the bells worked together to draw the people closer to God. The bells represented man's moving into God's presence, and the fruit made that presence soothing. It is readily apparent that great potential exists for community transformation if every believer would recognize their true identity in Jesus as someone on mission when helping children who need a stable loving family.

Not only does the identity of abused and neglected children need to change, but also the identity of Christ followers needs to change as well. For example, in Matthew 14:26-33, when Peter stepped out of the boat, he was afraid of the figure coming toward him. He was not sure it was the Lord, and therefore tested the situation by putting his life in danger. Jesus asks every believer today not to be afraid when a situation that seems confusing or unclear presents itself. That situation could be Jesus calling. It could be the very mission Christ has for His people, and He merely wants His followers to step out of the boat of their comfortable lives. The better we know Christ and His mission, the better we will recognize Him when he approaches us. We might recognize a foster child as someone who represents Jesus and His mission. The more we know the heart of the gospel, the more we will recognize it when we see it. Inviting an unrelated child into our lives may seem like a frightening situation, but we are told in Scripture that when we help a child, we are helping Jesus himself (Matt 10:42).

Jesus asks every believer today not to be afraid when a situation that seems confusing or unclear presents itself.

We cannot give up, even when the winds begin to blow. As believers, we have the power to live lives of peace, kindness, joy, and long-suffering, even when the winds of frustration come against us. We see in the story of the disciples in the storm (Matt 8:23-27) that even as they travel with Jesus, they are still crippled with fear.

The decision to foster or adopt may be one we are willing to do at first, but then challenging winds inevitably begin to blow. Believers of Christ can feel encouraged that they have the gifts and the fruit of the Spirit to calm or ride out the storms of life in the power of the Spirit. If we, like the disciples, invite a child into our homes and the winds blow, we can have confidence that Jesus is in our boat, so we do not need to be afraid.

If we, like the disciples, invite a child into our homes and the winds blow, we can have confidence that Jesus is in our boat, so we do not need to be afraid.

Unfortunately, many people are telling themselves a fear-based story. They are speaking a false narrative over themselves that says they will fail. False statements people tell themselves include thoughts such as: *We will never be able to let the child go home; we cannot afford it; our family will be hurt and damaged in some way if a foster child is a part of it.* They may even tell themselves that they will foster sometime in the future after they have "kids of their own," therefore missing the opportunity God is setting before them. There are kids in need today that we are called to help who could be a part of our spiritual family through salvation as we live the gospel in front of them every day. The true narratives are there, waiting to be fulfilled. In many cases, the fear that people experience is merely a manifestation of a false narrative that needs to be transformed by the truth of the gospel.

Romans 8 - God Makes His "Spirit of Adoption" Available

As a part of his pneumatology—and as a part of our pneumatology here of foster care and adoption—Paul describes in Romans 8 the spirit of adoption. It is important to examine the activity of the Spirit in relation to adoption and its connectedness to foster care because children in American foster care may face the reality of adoption at some point in their journey. This expository analysis will uncover the various aspects the Spirit plays in adoption theology.

Paul believed that the love of God was displayed and made

available through Christ to all the world by adoption into God's Kingdom, being made one with Jesus through the Spirit.[2]

Because of God's adoptive love for us we are compelled to love others.

Paul describes the spirit of adoption in Romans 8 and makes the case that it is through the work of the Spirit that people not only can "put to death the deeds of [their] sinful nature," but they are driven to love one another. Put another way, because of God's adoptive love for us (making us "children of God" as seen below), we are compelled to love others.[3]

> Therefore, dear brothers and sisters, you have no obligation to do what your sinful nature draws you to do, for if you live by its dictates, you will die. But if through the power of the Spirit you put to death the deeds of your sinful nature, you will live. For all who are led by the Spirit of God are children of God (Rom 8:12-14, NLT).

Verse 14 speaks explicitly to the way the spirit of adoption functions as a core feature of God. The Apostle Paul uses the term *adoption* (*huiothesia*) five times (Rom 8:15, 23; 9:4; Gal 4:5; and Eph 1:5). The first time, in verse 15:

> So you have not received a spirit that makes you fearful slaves. Instead, you received God's Spirit when he adopted you as his own children. Now we call him, "Abba, Father" (Rom 8:15).

These verses lay the groundwork for the hope described a few verses later in the chapter:

> For the earnest expectation of the creation waiteth for the revealing of the sons of God. For the creation was subjected to vanity, not of its own will, but by reason of him who subjected it, in hope that the creation itself also shall be delivered from the bondage of corruption into the liberty of the glory of the children of God (Rom 8:19-21, ASV).

Through the spirit of adoption, there is hope that the children of God will participate in freeing people from the bondage and corruption of this world through Christ. The Spirit of adoption is a new start, a new beginning, and a new hope for all people including foster children who need a loving, stable home.[4] Paul's goal is to make the case that adoption is relevant to each believer, because it is through spiritual adoption that we gain our inheritance from God.

The spirit of adoption is gospel because it tells believers who they are in relationship to God.

According to Scripture, it is not readily apparent to us that we have a great inheritance waiting for us.[5] We need some reminding. As Russell Moore notes, "We walk this path to maturity, the path Jesus walked before us."[6] Paul had to remind the believers in Romans 8 that there indeed is an inheritance waiting for them because sometimes it is not obvious. In this way, the spirit of adoption is gospel because it tells believers who they are in relationship to God. The spirit of adoption is also our mission in life because it compels us to help the marginalized and fatherless.[7] The believer in Christ is free to offer love and acceptance to others even at a great cost because they already have everything, they need in the life to come. The foster care and adoption connections here are powerful because, unfortunately, Christians can sometimes lose sight of this. We can be prone to live our lives in ways that suggest we have forgotten who adopted us. Furthermore, believers are prone to keep striving for significance and material balance even though we already have all we need the moment we are spiritually adopted in Christ. Moore says it very simply, "As Christians; we need to live like children and not like orphans."[8] As we become more aware of the spirit of adoption, we begin to understand the gospel more.[9] Therefore, when the church embraces foster care and adoption as a missional activity, it demonstrates what Christ did for each one of us on a spiritual level. In this way, the church will live out the life of Christ to our world.

The Spirit of adoption is a new start, a new beginning, and a new hope for all people including foster children who need a Loving, stable home.

The unified, agape love language Paul uses in Romans 8 is in stark contrast to the cultural language of today. By some, foster children are referred to as not being one of the "real" children of the family. It is assumed that couples consider adoption only after they could not have their "own" children. The spirit of adoption is a paradigm shift in how to define family. No longer is the biological line the primary connection, but rather it is the spiritual line that makes us family.

The spirit of adoption can also be seen in the illustration of water baptism. For instance, Romans 6 describes the connection of sin, salvation, and baptism; then in Romans 8 the concept of becoming a child of God is presented.[10] The similarity is that baptism brings together the relationship between children, parents, and community because the Father adopts us into His Kingdom and makes us His children in the presence of the community.[11] Therefore, we see that "Foster, adoptive and biological care of children are seen in the same theological light of baptism, as one in which God entrusts the care of children to family and community."[12]

Hoekema describes God's adoption as "an act of God's free grace, whereby we are received into the number and have a right to all the privileges of the sons of God."[13] Justification happens when God as our Father in heaven adopts us as his children. There is a redemptive action to adoption, and because the mission of God is to redeem His creation unto himself, the act of spiritual adoption is the motive to redemption. The following Scripture in 1 John restates what Paul is saying in Romans 8 with an emphasis on being in God's family:

> How great is the love the Father has given us so freely! Now we can be called children of God. That is who we are! The world does not know us because it did not know him. Dear friends, now we are children of God. He still hasn't let us know what we will be. However, we know that when Christ appears, we will be like him. We will see him as he is (1 John 3:1, NIRV).

The connection of spiritual and physical adoption to God is that He uses adoption to establish an intimate relationship with His people. Salvation, according to Romans 8:15 and 1 John 3:1, is based on God adopting people into the kingdom of God through Jesus Christ and saving them from sin. After this adoption is final in the hearts of people and God, there is power that comes from the Holy Spirit to change the world.

In the same way, the body of Christ continues God's saving work by adopting children into their physical family. This act of love models the same act of love that God offers His people through Jesus. In this way, adoption is not just biblical but part of God's redemptive plan for creation.

In the same way, the body of Christ continues God's saving work by adopting children into their physical family. This act of love models the same act of love that God offers His people through Jesus. In this way, adoption is not just biblical but part of God's redemptive plan for creation.

Then, in Romans 8:23 we see Paul connect our identity as God's adopted children to an eschatological concept. There is a deposit of the Spirit in verse 23:

> And we believers also groan, even though we have the Holy Spirit within us as a foretaste of future glory, for we long for our bodies to be released from sin and suffering. We, too, wait with eager hope for the day when God will give us our full rights as his adopted children, including the new bodies he has promised us (Rom 8:23, NLT).

Paul is saying that spiritual adoption is something we have today but also something we will have when we die. Being a son or a daughter of God means waiting for the full inheritance that will be given to us one day in heaven. Only because of our adoption into the family of God can we eagerly wait for this day. David Dockery in the *Holman Concise Bible Commentary* calls this day "God's plan of redemptive suffering moving toward fulfillment at the end of the age."[14] Adoption is God's mechanism that allows us to be in a new family, the family of God. It allows us to be royalty because we are in the kingdom of God. It allows us to live as royalty and not as an orphan any longer because we now know that we have a Father in heaven who will provide for all we need both on earth and in heaven. This is the gospel, and when we foster and adopt children into our families, we are acting as an extension of the gospel of Jesus Christ.

The Heart of the Gospel

According to Katerina Westerlund in her article, "Adoption as Spiritual Praxis in Individual Times," the theme of adoption would benefit from more theological exploration. Traditionally, it has focused on justification, sanctification, faith and calling, but recently more research on adoption as an independent theology of Christian living has taken place. This theology is a practical perspective that comes from the Hebrew Bible as its origin and calls for the care of orphans as well as the whole community of faith.[15] Westerlund goes on to explain how if God is seen as all controlling, then human beings will view Him as a competitor for control. Likewise, if God is omnipotent and seems hidden in human life, then people will seek to make their own order. However, adoption is the best of both extremes because God is seen as needed for freedom and acting in love to make freedom a reality.[16]

Therefore, it is conceivable that by doing the saving work Jesus is asking us to do in caring for orphans, we are at the very heart of His redeeming work.

The concept of adoption can be found throughout both Old Testament and New Testament books. Christ followers are clearly commanded to care for orphans as they live out the gospel of Christ. The mission of God, as stated by Michael Gorman in his book, *Becoming the Gospel*, is to redeem the world from sin.[17] Therefore, it is conceivable that by doing the saving work Jesus is asking us to do in caring for orphans, we are at the very heart of His redeeming work. Orphans are a people group who are marginalized and in need of being saved. They need a voice, and Jesus declares in Luke 4:17-21 when He begins His ministry that He has come for that very mission. There, Jesus unrolls the scroll of Isaiah 61 and reads from it, claiming to be the one sent to proclaim good news to the poor, restore sight to the blind, and set the captives free. He then begins His ministry in Galilee where most Jews were poor. His message was to follow him and be a child of God with all the rights, privileges, and inheritance granted as an adopted member of the Kingdom of God.

The Adoption of Moses

The historical argument for adoption can be traced as far back as the story of Moses. Kenneth Ngwa presents the idea of Exodus 2:1-10 as being more than merely a story about the adoption of one child. Moses represented the Hebrew people and was a young man. This dual representation offers interpretive insight into the greater Exodus story. He was rescued just as God would rescue the nation of Israel. Second, Moses being Hebrew was accepted into his Egyptian family despite vast cultural differences, like God accepting Israel as his adopted son.

Additionally, the adoptive mother mimics the actions of the biological mother in caring for Moses. This foreshadowing suggests an inside-out change where the nation followed God's people. The princess goes down to the place of the child, hears the cry of the child, and with the help of the local ethnic culture, adopts the child. There is also a similarity, according to Ngwa, in the consistency of how there is usually a middle person involved when adoption is concerned. There is a child or nation to be saved, a God doing a saving work, and someone with compassion willing to step in the middle. We see this when families foster or adopt a child. We also see this when Jesus stands in the middle for us, so God also can rescue and adopt us.[18] A father and son relationship is intimate, stable, and the forever family God had in mind. Adoption is full of dignity and worth pursuing if a child needs rescue. Several biblical characters, including Moses and Jesus himself, were adopted and used by God to save His people.

The Spirit of Adoption Redefines the Family

Mark 3 adds a second profound layer of purpose to adoption theology with a statement from Christ about who His family actually is. Not only is adoption the way we all have a relationship with God, and therefore worthy of replicating towards others in need, but being a part of the body of Christ is a new kinship. It is a new order of the family that places the brotherhood of believers higher in value and eternal in nature than human physical bloodlines. That means that when a child is adopted, a new family order is created, and if that child decides to accept Christ someday, he or she will be a part of the eternal body of Christ. The adoptee will indeed be a child of God and part of his forever family.

The traditional biological family in any society may fear becoming more complex, messy, and disorganized after adopting a new member of the family. What if the child does not get along well with the existing family? What if the adoptee is difficult to raise and discipline? What if life is harder as a result of this decision? These are all legitimate questions families need to work through, but when viewed through the eyes of Jesus, we see things differently. He accepted us with all our imperfections, and we should do the same for others. There is always a chance life could become more complicated, but the experience of thousands of adoptive parents and faithfulness of God suggest that life could also be more purposeful and rewarding. In God's eyes, this new family order receives his full blessing just as a nuclear family does, and in that we have much to anticipate.

Dan Cruver also talks about how a spiritual family is a part of who God is in his article, "Equipping the Generations: Adoption is bigger Than You Think. He describes how there is a father and son relationship that existed long before the universe was ever created, and the Holy Spirit is the bond in that relationship. Cruver describes the father and son relationship with Jesus that God gives to us on earth when he says,

> Simply put, the universe came into being out of a great love story. In the virgin's womb, this love touched down in the midst of our darkened broken world. The incarnate God showed his sacred face in the infant Jesus so that we could now enter this love. He tasted the sorrow of this world so that we might be taken into the joy of the eternal love of the Father and the Son.[19]

In this, we see the model of father and son as the basis for a healthy, loving, long-term family relationship. Cruver adds that when God created the world, He expanded His family by billions of children through a work of adoption. The surprising fact of this work is that the participants are empowered to participate in the mission of God and are not merely taken over by it. Jesus gives significant purpose to orphan ministry because it was His mission to redeem creation and that includes "the removal of the word orphan from the human vocabulary."[20] The pursuit of this mission is the central objective of orphan ministry.

Conclusion to Part Two

In Part Two, the heart of God for the vulnerable is on display. We see both in Old and New Testaments that caring for vulnerable children even to the point of adoption into our families is at the very heart of God's redemptive work. Therefore, foster care and adoption efforts by Christ followers is not a new idea but has been part of God's plan from the beginning. Every time we obey these directives from Scripture, we fulfill God's promises to care for the vulnerable in our world. We are being used by God to answer the prayers of those who do not have hope. We are used by God, as His Church, to keep His promises. It is an awesome responsibility and privilege, and the world takes notice when we show the love of the gospel. It always has.

PART THREE

Gaining a Greater Perspective

Part Three explores several factors that have influenced foster care ministry in the local church. Various voices provide a greater perspective to the way foster care has been addressed historically up to today in the church and society. All these influences help provide a backdrop for the landscape of foster care in American culture and shed light on the current opportunity the church must be the gospel in a way that is close to the heart of God.

This historical overview briefly examines how the church and society have addressed orphans in generations gone by to gain perspective on what has been accomplished, what has failed, and possibly what still needs to change.

I also review methods of local churches, parachurch organizations, and bridge organizations to gain insight into some of the ways that today's Christian culture is attempting to care for foster children in every American community.

The following chapter overviews problems related to the current realities in foster care and concerns for vulnerable children but also shows how successful reunification can play a significant role in restoring balance to a child's life, especially with culturally-appropriate and trauma-informed care.

CHAPTER 10

Historical Status of Orphans

The intent of this chapter is to provide several examples in history of how infants were viewed. It is not intended to be a comprehensive walk through every century or historical period but simply to provide a few examples that help provide a historical context.

To understand the calling of the church in helping orphans today, it is helpful to gain perspective on how orphans were cared for in a historical context. What seems clear when looking at the biblical narratives is that foster care and adoption are carried out in a very different manner today than they were in ancient times.[1] Despite these differences, there are undergirding theological principles that transcend time and culture. For example, when it comes to the idea of foster care, adoption, or biological parenting, the concept of caring for children in Christian theology comes from the belief that we are made children of God.[2]

Status of Orphans in Old Testament Times

The Hebrew culture of the Old Testament does not have a specific word to describe foster care or adoption in the way we use these terms today.[3] The relationship of a child legally was never changed in this culture because of the strong connection to the creation story. Therefore, if an orphaned child needed care, an extended family member would enter into an informal agreement that looked similar to the modern-day foster care structure because adoption was not thought to be as pleasing to God as being fruitful and multiplying. In this scenario, the biological parents continued as the legal parents, and extended family members provided care.[4]

Status of Orphans in the First to Fourth Centuries CE

In the New Testament, however, there was a new order introduced by Christ. Salvation through Jesus provided the mechanism of spiritual adoption as a way for people to enter the kingdom of heaven and paved the way for orphan adoptions to be accepted and encouraged by the church. The Early Church now believed that adoption was pleasing to God and began to fight the trends of culture that were destroying orphaned children.

During antiquity, the Early Church was vocal in their stance against abandonment because the Romans viewed adoption as an event impacting wealth and power. The word *adoption* comes from the Latin phrase "to choose for one's self" and was initially considered a legal proceeding to determine an heir.[5] Greek and Roman cultures were known for legal proceedings to assign rights for the passing down of property. The cultural norm was to assume that if the biological parents did not hold a newborn child, the child was to be abandoned. However, if a family desired to adopt a non-biological child, they would use the same procedure of holding the child during a legal ceremony with biological parents usually present. This process assumed that the biological family would stay in contact with the new caregiving parents.[6] However, history has shown that this has not always been possible or desirable.

In the Roman culture of the second to fourth centuries, infants that were not viewed as having a healthy future were placed out in the elements where they would typically die from exposure and neglect. Many times, these were girls or infants that had a congenital disability. The Romans would typically do this in the first few days of life so that it was viewed as more humane. This was widely practiced by Roman culture but was opposed by the Stoics as well as those following Christianity. Disapproval seemed to grow over time as the Christians continued to oppose this practice on a moral basis.

Moral lines are often crossed in culture when proper justification has been identified for a controversial issue. We see this in the second and fourth centuries when the Roman culture allowed the killing of newborn babies and called it infant exposure. Proverbs 14:12 and 16:25 warn us that there is a way that seems right to man, but its end is the way of death.[7] Infant exposure may be considered a way that seems right to humankind but is opposed by God. "Anthropologists have collected a considerable amount of material which shows that infanticide was a common phenomenon of primitive community life."[8] This practice was intended to control the population growth in a family by placing their newborns out in the elements to die or to be adopted by another family. It is interesting to note that this practice can be found even farther back in history than Roman times and was also associated with the ancient Greeks. The following paragraphs illustrate the position of the Greeks.

In his "Life of Lycurgus," the Greek historian Plutarch (A.D. 48-122) records that in Sparta in ancient Greece, the Spartan elders examined all newborn babies and ordered that any who were not well built and sturdy be killed by leaving them in the bush at the foot of Mount Taygetus:

> Offspring was not reared at the will of the father, but was taken and carried by him to a place called Lesche, where the elders of the tribes officially examined the infant, and if it was well-built and sturdy, they ordered the father to rear it, and assigned it one of the nine thousand lots of land; but if it was ill-born and deformed, they sent it to the so-called Apothetae, a

> chasm-like place at the foot of Mount Taygetus, in the conviction that the life of that which nature had not well equipped at the very beginning for health and strength, was of no advantage either to itself or the state." Such newborns starved or froze to death or were eaten by wild animals.[9]

This type of thinking continued to be passed down through the generations and made its way into the Roman culture because the laws supported the notion that parents had paternal power over the newborn and could decide to do what they felt best with his or her life.[10] Tertullian said that this practice was openly performed in Rome until it was made illegal, and even then, it was done somewhat in secret.[11] Parents would use infant exposure for several practical reasons. First, it allowed the poor to reduce the number of mouths to feed.[12] Second, if the child was a girl, it reduced the poor from the dowry responsibility later in life.[13] Third, children with disabilities were exposed to relieve the parents from the burden of caring for them with no hope of future contribution to the family's economic situation.[14] The Twelve Tables law of that time required babies that had deformities to be killed by drowning.[15] In fact, "Malformed newborns were not regarded as human infants and were usually killed immediately after birth."[16] This was a well-known and common practice. Fourthly, it allowed the social status of families to remain intact when illegitimate children were conceived. Finally, it preserved the inheritance of the rich for their children by limiting the number of times it was divided.[17] For all these reasons, it is believed that infanticide accounted for up to 50 percent of all births.[18]

Specific characteristics were identified to guide parents in deciding what children they should keep or expose:

> Soranus of Ephesus taught in Rome in the 2nd century CE: 'The infant who is worth rearing will be distinguished by the fact that its mother spent the period of pregnancy in good health, for conditions

> which require medical care, also harm the fetus. Second, by the fact that it was born at the due time, best at the end of nine months, and if it so happens, later; but also, after only seven months, also by the fact that it is perfect in all its parts, members and senses … And by conditions contrary to those mentioned, the infant not worth rearing is recognized.[19]

Obviously, many children did not meet these criteria. They were then exposed in the wild areas, by a mountainside, where people rarely traveled.[20] This would, of course, lead to almost certain death.

There was another option in the exposure process that would give a more hopeful outcome. This second option was a location where parents could place their children which was much more visible. One such location was called the *lactoria columna*—a place anyone looking to adopt a child would go in hopes of finding a new addition to their family.[21] Parents who would abandon their children here would leave a token to indicate the family status from which they came in hopes of encouraging others to adopt their child.[22] They also used these tokens as a way of identifying them later on in life.[23] If the exposed child had clothes, it meant the parents wanted them to be adopted, but if they were naked, they did not want their child to survive.[24] There were many, however, who would take these exposed children and sell them into slavery, prostitution, or the life of a gladiator.[25] This rescuing of a child was motivated more out of a desire for profit than out of mercy and love.[26]

The concept of abandonment and harm had different meanings. "Abandonment is the voluntary and permanent relinquishing of control over children by natal parents, whether leaving them, selling them, or signing them over to others."[27] Infant exposure may have been viewed as abandonment, but not to the point of imposing harm in the minds of these second-century parents.[28] The word *expositio* implied removal, offering, or separation but did not specifically reference harm.[29] It is possible that the choice of this word was strategic in supporting this practice because it did not imply wrongdoing by the parent. If harm was to come to the child, it was thought to be an accident. Harm during exposure was viewed as accidental because the intent was thought to simply separate the child and if the public did not adopt the child in some way, then the disastrous outcome was not the fault of the parent. Their hands were clean with this line of thinking. The irony is that each child when exposed to climate, animals, and neglect, was subject to harm and death.

Many Christian writers expressed their opinion about the issue of exposure. Collectively, they helped turn the tide by addressing a social justice issue with a moral argument. Tertullian in his writing "Ad Nationes," described the way the pagan culture treated newborns in the years A.D. 150-220 when he said they were evading the law by not killing the newborn directly but instead setting it out to be exposed to the cold and wild beasts.[30] By presenting these thoughts, Tertullian was connecting infant exposure to a much crueler death than simple infanticide.

The Jewish and Christian cultures would treasure and value their children because of how they saw them through the lens of God.

Another writing that put infant exposure in the spotlight was when Clement of Alexandria (A.D. 150-212) wrote "Instructor," and referred to how absurd it seemed that Roman women seemed to care more for their pet birds than they did for children.[31] "And though maintaining parrots and curlews, they do not receive the orphan child; but they expose children that are born at home, and take up the young of birds, and prefer irrational to rational creatures."[32] There was a contrast in how the Christians viewed their newborns versus the way the Greeks and Romans did. The Jewish and Christian cultures would treasure and value their children because of how they saw them through the lens of God.[33] Children were viewed as a primary purpose of marriage and sex instead of a burden or an embarrassment. The church as an institution opened the monastery to exposed infants and children as a way of saving them from almost sure death. These children would then be brought up in the monastery without further control of the parents.[34] Parents would often have to pay a fee to the monastery to take their children, and that decision was irrevocable. The poor, however, could not make a payment, but the monastery took them in any way. The result of this compassion was that monasteries were overrun with children and struggled to care for them well.[35] On the positive side, monasteries were many times the only escape for children that would otherwise be sold into slavery or killed.[36] The monastery solution was again one small step forward but not the full answer to infant exposure. It was, however, a way for the church to participate in social justice.

The Christian Church was advocating for a cause that was both a social justice issue as well as a theological one.

There was no systematic objection to infant exposure before Christianity except for the embarrassment that was recorded from wealthy families regarding the way they were viewed socially.[37] Christians pointed out that infant exposure was a sign that the family had engaged in illicit sexual relations and broken the union of marriage.[38] This further fueled the movement to stop infant exposure. The Christian Church was advocating for a cause that was both a social justice issue as well as a theological one. The two issues were in alignment and thus were met with favor by the culture over time because the ancient Romans did care about their children at the core.[39] Nevertheless, they did not have a system of beliefs, laws, or public opinion that supported them. Constantine was the first Roman emperor who became a Christian and changed a law in the year 374, making it illegal to expose infants.[40] Then, hospitals that were for poor children and orphans were created by St. Ephraem, St. Basil, and St. John Chrysostom.[41]

Status of Orphans in the Nineteenth and Twentieth Centuries (UK/US)

George Muller Bristol lived from 1805 -1898 and was the founder of the Ashley Down Orphan Homes in Bristol, England. He was world-renowned for his strategy of merely praying for the material needs of orphans and then watching how God would provide. He wrote many stories about how he never asked for anything but only prayed, then the material needs were met for the orphanage. His influence led to the development of orphanages in Great Britain, North America, Asia, Africa, Latin America, and Europe.[42]

As early American society began to take form, the beliefs and treatment of the poor were influenced by migrants from England who helped establish the laws in U.S. institutions for years to come. In many ways, the systems used to care for the poor in America and England were very similar.[43] Orphanages were built in America and modeled after those in England to meet the missing need that existed in society for orphans. They were primarily privately funded at the beginning but gained public funding as they became more developed. While the experiences of the children varied in these institutions, many children did well and thrived because of the stability they provided.[44]

The Catholic orphan asylum organized by Sisters of Charity was built in 1817. This facility grew to 350 children by 1825 and did so with all private funding.[45] This infrastructure became challenging to scale, however, when the Cholera outbreak in New York began in the early nineteenth century. As a result, the increased numbers of orphans that needed help strained the support available from the Catholic community.[46] This burden of care influenced the expansion of orphanage development west as far as Kansas. For example, in 1867 the first Catholic orphanage west of the Mississippi was opened but soon experienced opposition by protestant groups that did not want their orphaned children cared for by the Catholic leadership. To facilitate this desire, the Protestant leaders received public funding to open their orphanage as well.[47]

Then, in 1871, the Martin Luther Orphan's home was established by the Lutheran community of believers to continue the effort and desire to care for the poor as an act of their faith.[48] Volunteer staffing for this type of institution was a challenge but did find that single women and widows were in an ideal stage of life to offer service to this effort.[49] These homes, therefore, marched forward with their mission for years to come.

The growing population of children in orphanage communities, however, arrived at a point in the early twentieth century that required new and innovative solutions for care.

From 1800 to 1900 the number of orphanages in the U.S. had grown from seven to 613 that housed 50,000 children. In 1853 Charles Loring Brace, a Methodist minister, formed the Children's Aids Society in New York. He was an American minister and early social work pioneer. He had an innovative idea to place poor and needy children in families out west instead of in big institutions in the city. To accomplish his idea, he embraced the cutting-edge transportation of his time—the steam locomotive. Trains were state of the art that time, and the orphan trains were the beginning of our current foster care system. This new idea was a way of addressing the failures in capacity, quality, and sustainability of the orphanage model. He is considered a father of the modern foster care movement.[50]

In the 1970s, a high number of foster children were sent to mental health facilities because of federal funding made available. Some foster children needed this care, but approximately 50 percent did not. Therefore, they were inappropriately housed in an institution rather than in a safe, loving family. The 1980s brought a reaction to this type of care called the "preservation movement" because thought leaders began supporting the fastest path to a permanent family. This permanency trend has continued in a variety of forms and is still impacting the foster care system today. As a result of this shift in focus from institutional care to outplacement family care, the foster care system has been provided with a federal budget that in 2016 was an estimated 60 billion dollars.[51]

Researchers, however, continue to seek answers about foster care effectiveness because funding is only a resource. The question still remaining is how effectively that funding is being used. As greater numbers of children enter the foster care system each year the methods of care are continuously under review. What is the best way to care for the orphans in American society today? The church is positioned to be that answer.

What is the best way to care for the orphans in American society today? The church is positioned to be that answer.

It seems logical then, that the Christian Church would be in the middle of the foster care chaos because it claims to have the answer that brings peace. The Prince of Peace not only wants to be found in peaceful places but also where peace is needed most. This means that the local church will need to participate in conversations where brokenness is found and outcomes of forgiveness, peace, and hope are desperately needed.[52]

The foster care crisis across the county is experiencing the type of chaos that needs a voice of peace. More children need homes in America than are available. Thus, church has an opportunity to step into this messy situation and bring peace by standing in the gap for children in foster care, social workers, and biological families. Together, church families can bring hope and peace to a part of the community that otherwise sees very little hope.

CHAPTER 11

Current Status of Foster Care

The following chapter overviews problems related to the current realities in foster care and concerns for vulnerable children but also shows how successful reunification can play a significant role in restoring balance to a child's life, especially with culturally-appropriate and trauma-informed care.

Numbers Tell the Story

The Annie E. Casey Foundation notes that "In 2020, 213,964 children under 18 entered foster care in the United States, a rate of 3 per 1000. Kids ages 1 to 5 make up the largest share (30% in 2020) of children entering care. A total of 407,493 children and youth were living in foster care in 2020."[1] Further, the Foundation notes that 48 percent of children are reunited with their parents each year, 10 percent live with a legal guardian, 6 percent live with relatives, and 9 percent age out of foster care by turning eighteen years of age.[2] Of those children that age out of the system, 29 percent become homeless by the time they are twenty-one years old and 20 percent are incarcerated by the time they are 21.[3]

These numbers seem to tell a story of how the current system needs to improve and strengthen its level of care so that foster children are better prepared to enter society as adults. These numbers also indicate that even with a large state and federal budget, only half of the children accomplish the goal of reunification. The other half lean on the help of the community or face the uncertain future of aging-out.

The Annie E. Casey Foundation publishes a booklet each year with data about the well-being of children in each state. Overall, they believe that "When communities are safe and have strong institutions, good schools, and quality support services, families and their children are more likely to thrive."[4] In this statement they are asking for the people in each community to work together to make things better for kids in need.

The Changing Nature of Childhood Itself

Neil Post writes his book about how childhood, as we know it in America, is only about 150 years old.[5] He believes that the printing press was the catalyst for creating a culture that defines childhood as the time spent under eighteen years of age. During this period of life, social, emotional, and educational development are prioritized over working to provide a living. Post believes that, in the same way the printing press redefined modern childhood expectations in our culture, current electronic media outlets are contributing to making it disappear. For example, young girls are seen in music videos and television programming with an adult identity, clothing, and vocabulary. He hopes that the distinction of childhood will not disappear but believes that American culture is "Hostile to the idea of childhood."[6] He points out that celebration of the American child's birthday only began a recently as the late eighteenth century, and that in 1890, 93 percent of children fourteen to seventeen years old were not in high school but rather in the adult workforce.[7] Things did change for the better, but if America is not careful, Post suggests that childhood will once again be forgotten and disappear.

Post believes that children are a "living message that we send to a time we will not see."[8] It is possible, he says, for society to exist without an identity for children and believes this is happening today in American culture, pointing to evidence of this such as crime increasing for children under fifteen years old, media models twelve to fifteen years old, and the distinctive types of dress that children wear at younger and younger ages.[9] Post states that the timeframe of 1850-1950 is the high point of what is called the distinction and value of childhood,[10] when the current stereotype of the American family was formed. However, ever since then it has been in decline. Post uses additional examples in his books such as childhood increases in drug use, alcoholism, and sexual activity as proofs for his theory that childhood is on the decline. He points to a physiological pattern as well:

> It has been claimed that the onset of puberty in females has been falling by about four months per decade for the past one hundred and thirty years, so that, for example, in 1900 the average age at which menstruation first occurred was approximately fourteen years, whereas in 1979 the average age was twelve years.[11]

Postman also points out that in today's media, children are hard to find on TV. Shows are mostly for adults with adults as the characters. Families are not as interesting in media any longer. He points out various Hollywood movies in his book that show children with habits and preferences no different than adults.[12] Disney is also losing its definition of what a child is to the works of Judy Blume and others who make teen literature more adult.[13] Therefore, it is suggested that those who are not in alignment with the moral majority of culture to, at this point, borrow from some of their memories.[14] In other words, Post highlights the essential role that religious moral conservatism has in valuing the innocence of children and that the passing on of these values to the next generation will be critical in avoiding further moral decline in our culture.

Poverty's Impact

Other concerns for vulnerable children stem from the impact of poverty in America. Mary Frances Bowley writes about the risk factors that increase the chances that children will be subject to abuse, neglect, and abandonment.[15] Her research has found two common trends in troubled adults that trace back to childhood. Careful consideration of these factors is critical to understand the challenges associated with caring for vulnerable children.

Poverty is one area of need in America that puts children in a vulnerable environment. The national poverty rate was 12.8 percent in 2021, but the child poverty rate was 16.9 percent.[16] These authors believe that stopping poverty can only happen when young mothers and fathers find employment that will support them.[17] This belief is founded on the belief that every mother and father with gainful employment will provide their vulnerable children with a secure financial foundation to build on. This employment can be accomplished through programs that promote self-awareness, skills development, resume writing, career matching, and professional dress. When one person helps a child, they can be the one who sets that child down a completely different path. When one person mentors a mother and/or father toward greater self-awareness and skills development, they also point them in a better direction in life.

Hunger affects one out of five children in America. It is another factor that puts children in vulnerable environments. "A young woman who has been living in the worst kind of slavery—right here in this country—tells her story and it includes 'I trusted him because I was hungry, and he was the only one who offered me anything to eat.'"[18] Not only is being hungry frustrating, sad, and painful, but it puts children in a vulnerable state of mind. They are open to following people they usually would not. They are vulnerable to exploitation and manipulation because they simply are starving. Hunger is unlike other problems in society in that it is hidden. People cannot tell someone is hungry. It is an unseen issue. As Bowley and Franklin depict,

> Hunger is trauma, and when food has been scarce, the after-effects can last a lifetime. It creates a survivor mentality, one that can manifest in food hoarding and distrust. Hungry children often exhibit emotional, developmental, and educational delays. They are disadvantaged in the classroom, which hurts their development during the critical years in school. Hungry children are often labeled with a learning disorder when the heart of the issue could be undernourishment. Education is the single greatest path out of generational poverty, and yet it is nearly impossible for children to latch on and make the most of it when they cannot focus on anything else but the loud growl of hunger in their bellies.[19]

However, when this basic need is met, children have a chance to develop and stand on solid ground. They can make better decisions and are not as vulnerable to those looking to use them in harmful ways. Fighting hunger addresses the vulnerability of children and also provides a way for the community to help. Providing food is a way to build relationships, bridge gaps in the community, and open doors for connecting people to employment opportunities.

The Goal of Reunification

The child welfare response to improved care for vulnerable children has embodied the belief that reunification should be the ultimate goal whenever possible. Adoption is, of course, a welcome solution for broken families who are unable to be reunited, but the general position of the Kenosha County Child Welfare Agency, for example, is to, whenever possible, help children remain with their biological families.

Interviews I conducted with the Kenosha County District attorneys' office, Kenosha County Juvenile Judge's office, and the Kenosha County supervisor's office at the Department of Health and Human Services, all consider reunification as the most desirable option for the child in most cases. Don Browning is a theologian who has spent many years following research showing that "Children generally do better when they are placed with intact families along the lines of biological models."[20] This perspective highlights the caution needed in viewing adoption as a superior and first choice solution when the glory of God can also be displayed through healing and reunification of families as well. Believers need to remain on the front lines to help families remain intact whenever possible.

Reunification is the most desirable option for the child in most cases.

Lisa Cahill echoes the warning of overvaluing adoption at the expense of other critical biological family preservation efforts. She writes about adoption from a Catholic perspective as she points out that adopted children often feel disconnected from their biological ties. Just because a child was adopted does not mean their desire to relate to their natural birth identity disappears.[21] This philosophy is what fuels advocates for open adoptions, the concept of adoptive parents staying connected with birth families as much as possible.

The pressure to place a child with an adoptive resource or return them home to their biological families is significant because the outcomes of children aging out of the welfare system are often tragic. Mathew M. LeClaire studied the likelihood of aged-out foster children to be engaged in criminal activity in 2014. He found that without stability and support structure, these children became young adults who were more likely to be homeless, drink alcohol, and experiment with drugs than other children their age.[22] It is interesting to note that even though this group of aged-out foster children is a relatively low number overall, they are a very high percentage of the people represented in the criminal justice system.[23]

The Call for Culturally Appropriate Care

Another voice of caution when aggressively promoting adoption comes from lessons learned from a study in New Zealand, according to Erica Neman in her article *History of Transracial Adoption.* There were significant differences between the way Europeans approached adoption and the way the natives of New Zealand approached the same issues. This led to the 1881 Adoption of Children Act and the learning of many guiding principles for adoption across social platforms. The natives of New Zealand had close family structures and did not see it acceptable to have strangers raise their children. Instead, they had relatives who would help raise their children in their absence or if they were unable. The nuclear family worked with the extended family to meet the needs of orphaned children. In this structure, the children kept their identity strong, and the relatives took on this responsibility with pride.

The unique characteristics of cultures should be considered when attempting to rescue a child from the broken situations in which they live.

This model had one primary concern: that the child was able to maintain their primary identity and retain knowledge of where they came from. The results were positive, but the motivating factors were misplaced. The natives believed that if their children were placed with strangers, they would be mistreated, and that was rarely the case.[24] Then, as history unfolded over the years and adoption became more accepted, another law was passed called the 1955 Adoption Act. This legislation made adoptions closed, and case files sealed. Children were not encouraged to seek out biological parents, and this is still the current law of the land. As was predicted, natives of New Zealand opposed the closed adoption system and were successful at creating a new open adoption system that was supported by the government for the placement of native children within their cultural family structures. The lesson learned was that the closed adoption system that was effective in other parts of the world was harmful to the natives of New Zealand. Therefore, globally, the unique characteristics of cultures should be considered when attempting to rescue a child from the broken situations in which they live.[25]

The Call for Trauma Informed Care

If children are to be reunited with their biological family, training for foster parents helps them successfully understand the needs of abused and neglected children. The foundation for this effort is the belief that improved training and expectation will translate to higher quality care for the children. Jane Schooler, Betsy Keefer Smalley, and Timothy J. Callahan write about the impact foster and adoptive children have on the families that have committed to care for them. They describe in their book various aspects of trauma and how proper expectation can help families be successful in the long run. One of the first expectations that must change in the opinion of these authors is how fostering or adoptive families assume love will be enough for a child who has suffered trauma.

Foster families assume that if enough love and care are provided, all the behavioral issues will melt away. The reality, however, is that love needs to be paired with practical knowledge of what to expect from a child who has experienced trauma.[26]

For this reason, families need to understand some of the signs of trauma and how to appropriately respond. The good news is that "Healing begins as parents see their role as external regulators for their children, working to increase pleasure and enhance attachment."[27] It can be hard because the stress of past trauma can stretch a family beyond parenting skills used in the past, but the reward for sticking with it is that healing is activated as healthy attachment begins. Healthy attachment ensures safety, and when that aspect of their lives is solid, all other aspects of development can take place.[28] Schooler, Smalley, and Callahan say that loving a traumatized child means embracing a love like no other. "It is love lived out every day in new and unfamiliar ways."[29]

Families need to understand some of the signs of trauma and how to appropriately respond.

There is great hope that being a foster or adoptive family can change a child's life. For example, "It is estimated that 50 percent of who we are is inherited. The other half is formed through experience."[30] This hope was woven throughout Schooler, Smalley, and Callahan's book with stories of real people who experienced challenges in adopting or fostering children at the beginning but pushed through and saw amazing change over time. It is this aspect of time that Schooler, Smalley, and Callahan emphasize in various chapters because the reality is that trauma takes time to heal. Parents may want to see change faster that it happens, but it *is* happening according to these authors. Patience and commitment are needed to see complete healing in a child's life because traumatized spirits are fragile. Even if the child is doing much better in a daily routine, there can be relapses connected to the trauma they experienced from time to time. Often these relapses are unforeseen and take everyone by surprise. They could be triggered by merely taking a promotion at work which requires moving to a new home. This move could be especially hard on the adopted child because it triggers the fears they had every time they moved around in foster care. These authors note that kids having experienced trauma have the following underlying feelings, which can lead to behavioral relapses even after great improvement has been made:

1. Experience themselves as inadequate and incomplete
2. Have a limited and fragmented sense of self and autonomy
3. Experience deep, obscure, and overwhelming shame
4. Have intense feelings of rage without an easily identifiable threat
5. Feel overwhelmed with pervasive anxiety, but without an identifiable threat
6. Experience overwhelming despair[31]

This list illustrates the broken framework of a child that has experienced trauma, abuse, or neglect. Random events or situations that seem reasonable in everyday life can trigger a behavioral outbreak even after strong attachment has occurred. Foster and adoptive parents should be prepared for this eventuality and not be discouraged. It is a regular part of the healing process. Despite persistent challenges, as healthy attachment is developed, the child will increasingly find comfort and healing in the security of their loving parent.[32]

Conclusion to Part Three

Every culture throughout history has wrestled with how it will address the needs of vulnerable children. Amazingly, when the church stepped in to help, the world took notice. The church has stepped in to take its rightful place in caring for vulnerable children in the past, and that door is open once again today. The entire American foster care system depends on love because it is an outplacement model. They need people to open their homes out of love for others or the entire system will fail. Think of how reliant our country is on plain old-fashioned love. Jesus said the world would know we are His disciples by our love for one another. So, with the door wide open for Christians to show love through foster care ministry, the time is now to rally together once again and change our country for Christ—one foster child at a time.

PART FOUR

Getting Involved

The goal of this book is to bring you to a point of getting involved. Therefore, Part Four will introduce you to some practical concepts, knowledge, and systems you can use to get involved as an individual or as a church ministry.

Part Four (in chapter 12) demonstrates the important role the local church plays and how it can help meet the needs of foster care and adoption today. It also introduces you to a successful local church model. This exciting model provides training for individuals to foster and adopt as well as local church training for congregations to provide support to those foster care families.

The final chapters in Part Four describe how I did a systematic examination of the need for foster care ministry at Journey Church in Kenosha, Wisconsin (chapter 13) and then how I evaluated the one-year implementation of that foster care ministry (chapter 14). As you read Journey Church's story, may God continue to remind you not only of His biblical mandate for caring for orphans and widows but also of His Spirit's empowerment to live out the gospel and the mission of God in your community.

As you look to become a foster parent or begin supporting foster families in your church, the impact of foster family support is more effectiveness with basic trauma-informed care education. Forbes and Post addressed the issue of foster care and adoption success in their book, *Beyond Consequences, Logic, and Control.* Their goal for this book was to bring new methodology to those parents who commit to raising a child that has suffered abuse, neglect, or abandonment. Forbes and Post believe that

> It is not about parenting "disturbed" or "hurt" or "unattached" children. It is not about stopping at every moment to "make" attachment a reality. Parenting a child with a traumatic history is about learning to interpret the child's reactions to past experiences from a place of compassion, understanding, and love. Love is enough when it is in the absence of fear. It takes seeing the child for whom he or she is and meeting the child in their pain.[1]

Interestingly, Forbes and Post say love is enough with the proper methods. The premise of their approach is letting go of control and fear in the name of love. They encourage foster and adoptive parents first to be willing to feel the pain of the child and then take on that pain with the child.

This aspect is similar to the love of Jesus and how He was willing to feel pain and take on the pain of sinners for the sake of healing and restoration. In this way, Forbes and Post suggest that the act of taking on the pain of the child is an extension of the gospel. Their parenting methods are controversial to some because they are counter-intuitive.[2] They believe that when the motive is love, the actions of releasing control produce healthy attachment, and that attachment soothes the soul, leading to improved behavior. However, releasing control takes courage because it seems irresponsible to forgive stealing, lying, and hoarding of food on the spot without any consequences. Common sense tells a parent to include consequences with wrong actions. However, instead of fear-based consequences, Forbes and Post subscribe to the opposite, teaching that traumatized children are seeking external ways to regulate internally.[3] Since the child has trouble internally regulating themselves, their poor behavior makes them feel better. They get a good feeling from stealing or lying. It can be an addictive behavior because the body releases similar chemicals when lying as are released with heroin or cocaine.[4] These negative behaviors make the child feel good, which is why punishments are not effective. Forbes and Post say that if a parent punishes a child for stealing, it is possible for the child to steal an item soon after because the child is not stealing to be disobedient; the child is stealing to feel good. Repetition of stealing and lying also creates a subconscious response to stress. When a child is feeling stressed, they turn to what makes them feel good.[5]

Mary Frances Bowley and Jennifer Bradley Franklin in *Make it Zero* present many connected aspects contributing to adults that are dysfunctional and vulnerable. The authors studied abused women and concluded that most of the women in shelters of some kind as an adult suffered abuse or neglect as a child. Therefore, the authors have set out to change the world one person at a time by inspiring everyone to do something to help abused and neglected children.[6] The big goal for this book is to see all poverty, hunger, isolation, abuse, and trafficking reduced to zero. Her simple plan is to inspire one person to start working with one more person to help vulnerable children. She believes that as this cycle of working together continues; the dream of zeroing out these problems is possible, writing,

> I have seen a common theme emerge most victimized adults were vulnerable when they were children. It has been with this realization that if we correct the factors that lead to childhood vulnerability, we can make a difference in the lives of those children and the lives of the adults they will grow up to be.[7]

Russell Moore addresses the issue church leaders face when attempting to know how to begin creating a ministry for orphans in the church. He writes a portion of his book, *Adopted for Life: The Priority of Adoption for Christian Families and Churches*, applying adoption theology to the local church and provides a possible roadmap for churches to use in beginning their adoption ministry. He first suggests that churches create a culture of adoption through preaching from the pulpit.[8] Culture creation is vital because creating a culture starts with communicating the type of change a church wants to see. Preaching about adoption theology answers the question of "why" behind the actions that will follow. The people hear the heart of the leader on the subject as well as the voice of the God through the reading of the text. The Holy Spirit then uses this time of culture creation to stir the hearts of the people and align them with the will of God. The role of the communicator in preaching about adoption theology is ultimately to create an adoptive-missional church.[9] There is a synergistic effect that happens when the local church begins to catch the adoptive vision for their community. Christians begin to make the connection of how reaching the world with the gospel and helping orphans are connected. Not every person can open their home to a child, but everyone can do something.

Kathryn Purvis, David Cross, and Wendy Sunshine collaborated to produce a book called *The Connected Child: Bring Hope and Healing to Your Adoptive Family* that speaks of the power compassion plays in caring for orphans:

> Compassion will help you be tolerant of a child's deep neediness, and to be forgiving when he or she does not understand something that seems so basic, like how to sit at a dining room table with a family, how to use toilet paper, or how to read people's facial expressions.[10]

Jesus had compassion on the marginalized of His time. He also has compassion for us today. It is compassion that allows us to understand what others have been through and empathize with others to the point of getting involved. Real compassion is not stationary or just feeling bad for someone but rather jumps into action to help someone in need. Purvis, Cross, and Sunshine put it this way when speaking about neglected children:

> The lives that many of them have endured were more difficult than we can fathom. With compassion, parents can look inside the child's heart and recognize the impairments and deep fear that drive maladaptive behavior—fears of abandonment, hunger, being in an unfamiliar environment, losing control, and being hurt.[11]

It is this compassion that aligns our expectations to a realistic level. We can express the fruit of the Spirit when caring for children who do not trust adults or who have never had healthy attachment before. Compassion …

- demonstrates love
- compels us to be joyful and celebrate the moments when a child does the smallest thing right
- puts others first and us second
- spurs us on to be faithful when we feel like giving up or being kind when a child yells at us in frustration

As Purvis, Cross, and Sunshine observe, "Deep down, these children want desperately to connect and succeed but don't understand how. As parents, it is our job to show them."[12] These authors call compassion our touchstone.[13] It is love, and love is the thesis of God's Word.

CHAPTER 12

Foster Family Support

The Need is Great

Katarina Westerlund writes about the motive of adoption in our culture and says that the way we understand and relate to children has profoundly changed over time. She points out a noticeable shift that has occurred, from the culture of previous centuries where parents considered children as a source of meaning in their lives, to a twenty-first century culture of individualism and autonomy.[1]

Sheryl Ryan cites that in 2004 the rate of inter-country adoption was at its peak of 40,000 adoptions worldwide to help the thirteen million global orphans who had lost both parents in their lives. After this point, however, inter-country adoptions decreased by half because of three issues. First, countries in Africa, East Europe, and Russia and China started to push back against their children being removed from their culture and language. Second, sex trafficking was taking place under the guise of finding better homes for children. Third, as adoptions decreased, the Christian Alliance for Orphans (CAFO) became a major role-player in the USA to promote the adoption of tens of thousands of children in foster care who were available for adoption. This led to books, films, and conferences aimed at motivating Christians to take up the cause of adoption and foster care once again in the American communities of faith.

Foster children often do not have a parent, relative, or friend able or willing to care for them. They need a safe place until a foster home can be identified. Once a foster home is found, these children wait until permanence can be accomplished. Some children return to their biological parent while others find permanence through adoption. However, others never find permanence and turn eighteen without any family to call their own. These children are at increased risk of homelessness, incarceration, and become targeted victims of human trafficking.

There are children in our country and around the world who need a safe home, but most local churches are not even in the game.

The need is great, but statistics show that the majority of Protestant churches in America are not engaging this issue; for example, one survey done by LifeWay Research in 2018 found that 60 percent of churchgoers reported their churches were not involved in foster care or adoption ministry in any way during the past year.[2] This meant that not even one person at their church was involved or talking about the issue in the past year. One person is all it would have taken to put their church on the list. To make matters worse, only 12 percent of churches reported having leader who spoke of it from the platform.[3] There are children in our country and around the world who need a safe home, but most local churches are not even in the game. The culture needs the church. The church needs to help.

Foster care is a critical stage for vulnerable children because it is at this point that they may be separated from their family forever or be reunited—with a grand celebration! It is also the point in their lives that families of faith can influence broken lives and fill them with discipleship opportunities 24/7. If the church says *yes* to this opportunity, doors open to breaking generational cycles of poverty, neglect, and abuse, and identity begins to be shaped for children as to who they indeed are in Christ.

Also, biological parents often open their hearts to the foster family for discipleship as well, because a relationship begins to form as a child is lovingly cared for out of love for Christ. Jesus came to bind up the brokenhearted. This is our mission, and the Holy Spirit has empowered us to make it a reality.

The Church as the Solution

The church seems uniquely positioned in today's culture to have an answer for what James 1:27 calls us to—that true religion is to help the widows and the orphans. This is not an option or a suggestion but a *command* that demonstrates *love*. When the Early Church cared for the orphans, they were caring for widows as well because in biblical times the two were often found together. Today, we often see single mothers at risk of losing their children because of substance abuse or a variety of other issues. Therefore, a case can be made that single moms and foster children are a type of modern day widow and orphan of America. This argument can also be connected to the problematic reality that America has many programs and funding for the elderly but little for the care of a single mother. Also interesting is the fact that James 1:27 calls every Christian to care for the orphan but does not call every believer to bring a child into their home. The call is for everyone to *do something*. Therefore, the opportunity for the church today is to facilitate ministry that promotes, supports, and invites more people to support the care of vulnerable children.

Even secular studies have shown that religious teaching in the lives of the poor leads to more productive living. Most researchers have found that religiosity reduces substance abuse, increases self-control, health, education, and social connectedness in those living in poverty.[4]

Put another way, when the lives of children are disrupted, torn apart, and neglected, they need someone to help. When their parents are hurting, frustrated, and confused, they also need help. Ephesians 3:8-10 describes God's plan for a holy nation, a royal priesthood to come to their aid. The church of Jesus Christ is designed and positioned to help the broken-hearted and the vulnerable in every community.[5] This response not only provides answers to those foster children and biological parents in need but also demonstrates to a skeptical world that God loves them.[6]

James 1:27 calls every Christian to care for the orphan but does not call every believer to bring a child into their home.

Church leaders have an opportunity to play an influential role in the foster care and overall orphan care conversation. To learn what pastors of Assemblies of God churches across the country know about the issue, The Assemblies of God Family Services Agency surveyed church leaders in 2013 and found that only 49 percent of pastors were aware of the foster care crisis in America.[7] Some encouraging news, however, was that 47 percent of the pastors surveyed indicated they would be willing to prioritize orphan care ministry as one of the top three ministries in their church *if they only knew how.*[8]

Moore suggests that churches create a culture of foster care and adoption through preaching from the pulpit.[9] This is key because creating a culture starts with communicating the type of change a church wants to see. Preaching about adoption theology answers the question of 'why' behind the actions that will follow. The people hear the heart of the leader on the subject as well as the voice of God through the reading of the text. The Holy Spirit then uses this time of culture creation to stir the hearts of the people and align them with the will of God. The role of the communicator in preaching about adoption theology is to create an adoptive-missional church.[10]

The call is for everyone to *do something*. Therefore, the opportunity for the church today is to facilitate ministry that promotes, supports, and invites more people to support the care of vulnerable children.

There is a synergy that happens when the local church begins to catch the adoptive vision for their community. Christians begin to make the connection between reaching the world with the gospel and helping orphans. Not every person can open their home to a child, but everyone can do something. When people adopt a child from Russia, they gain a heart and burden for the people of Russia. Likewise, when a family fosters a child or adopts a child from their local community, they develop a burden and a heart for the people of their community. When Christians develop a love for a group of people, the potential to impact them would seem very high.[11]

Moore also describes an effective orphan care ministry consisting of the following components:

> 1. A local church could organize meals for adoptive parents. 2. Parent classes could be created that address adoptive parent challenges. 3. Childcare could be provided for adoptive families or new mothers to free them up for other activities. 4. Baby dedications could be augmented to now be called child dedications, thus allowing adopted children to be celebrated as well. 5. Local businesses could be contacted to donate funds to an adoption fund to make it easier for families to take the next step in the adoption process. 6. Lists could be provided of agencies available, home study specialists, and ballpark costs involved with different types of

> adoptions. 7. Prevention classes could be organized for pregnant mothers to provide options and hope they otherwise are without. 8. Lists of attorneys that offer free services for adoption cases could be prepared and made available as needed. 9. Prayer teams could be assembled for the entire adoptive process.[12]

These ideas are practical ways the local church could make an impact and make adoption and foster care a priority in the community. All of the ideas outlined by Moore can be done for foster parents as well. They need all the same levels and aspects of support. This proposed model of orphan care is formed out of a theology that views adoption and foster care as the gospel as well as missional.

Local churches of today promote foster care and adoption because the church can provide children with a bridge to the world of the potential foster care or adoptive parent. They need someone to show them the right way by modeling good behaviors. Karyn Purvis describes the opportunity the local church has to help a child heal when an adverse scenario occurs: "You have a unique opportunity to change that scenario by building a bridge to the world for your at-risk adoptive children. You and the rest of your family can become a safe-haven and an ally, eager to share their concerns."[13] Helping change the life of a child can be as simple as creating a safe place for them that allows for attachment to occur.

Another study that supports the potential impact the church can have on foster care and adoption was carried out in 2015 by Mathew Scott Thompson. This study revealed that supportive religious communications and personal relationships with adoptive families ranked highest as factors influencing new families to adopt for the first time. The rankings for both tied with a score of 88.9 percent out of a possible 100.[14] These results would suggest the church has a relevant and timely voice in speaking to the foster care crisis of American culture today.

Conclusion

There is a great need for supporting foster families and foster children. Many of those children will need an adoptive home. Foster families are often the first option and the greatest chance of stability for a child. The Christian home, therefore, becomes a discipleship center for vulnerable children to receive love, support and to see Jesus lived out right in front of them every day.

But of course, not everyone can be a foster parent. So, the body of Christ has an amazing opportunity to simply support the foster parents who can. With simple acts of love and support, foster families stay in the game longer and stand in the gap longer for foster children until a permanent home is identified. Everyone truly can do something to help—even if it is just writing a note of appreciation to show you care.

CHAPTER 13

Local Church Pilot Program:

This chapter describes the story of establishing foster family support at Journey Church, specifically the detailed steps taken to identify the need for a system of foster care ministry.

How We Began

Journey Church is located between the two international cities of Chicago and Milwaukee in the Southeast region of Wisconsin. Each weekend Journey Church is host to over three thousand attendees in four locations. The largest location is located in the city of Kenosha, where the church operates its foster care ministry.

The American foster care system needs help caring for the approximately 400,000 children per year that do not have a permanent safe home.[1] At the time of this writing, Kenosha, Wisconsin had 197 of that total number, and eighty-five of those children still required placement into a foster home.[2] Kenosha County continually seeks qualified families to provide a temporary and safe place for foster children to live to help keep up with the demand for homes.[3]

Fourty-seven percent of pastors surveyed by the Assemblies of

God Compact Services reported that they would add foster care ministry into the top vision initiatives of their church if they only knew how.[4] Similarly, the Christian Alliance for Orphans reported that 38 percent of churchgoers are interested in being foster parents, but only 1 percent follow through with the process.[5] In both cases, a significant gap exists between pastors and congregation members from which interest translates into action.

To address this need, I determined to learn more about how the local church could close those gaps with an effective compassionate care system and to evaluate the impact and theological alignment of foster parent support activities. Specifically, I planned to examine the strengths of a support system and analyze the solutions it presents. The dropout rate for foster parents after one year without any support is perceived to be significant, but its exact impact is unknown. Therefore, a healthy support program offered the hope of substantially lowering the foster parent dropout rate at Journey Church.

A System of Care for the Local Church

In the support model, a local church leader is asked to evaluate the landscape of foster care in their community and create a ministry plan that suggests a variety of action steps for the upcoming year. It is assumed that because each church will have a unique ministry context, it will be best served to evaluate and apply ministry solutions accordingly. The following are suggested areas of focus that could be addressed:

Advocacy

Media campaigns to raise awareness (CAFO, http://cafo.org/nfci). This resource includes many domestic and international organizations, podcasts, and campaign ideas for local church leaders looking to do something to help children in foster care. One such effort is Orphan Sunday. This syndicated campaign organized by the Christian Alliance for Orphans is recognized by churches each year to promote awareness for foster care and adoption in their local church. Churches invite social services in to talk about the need in the community and answer questions after a service to interested families. Small focus groups can be formed with friends in the church to answer questions and be a support in the decision-making process.

Service Projects

Churches may find meeting physical needs of foster parents an easy place to begin. Project examples might include packing backpacks for social services to give foster parents at the time of placement or clothing donated through a local foster closet organization. Families might also find simple tasks like writing thank you cards for foster parents especially rewarding and easy to do. Just letting a foster parent know what they are doing matters and that they are appreciated will have a significant impact. One national organization that helps connect churches to the needs of the foster families is called CarePortal.

Recruitment

Some organizations focus on this step of the process by helping to recruit foster families and point them to agencies for licensing. A few of these organizations would include: www.backyardorphans.org or http://www.cherishkids.org/.

Volunteer Management

At this step volunteers are organized to support various aspects of the foster care cycle from prevention to adoption when it becomes available.

Prevention

Safe Families (https://safe-families.org/) works with churches to help prevent children from entering foster care. Local chapters work with social services to help families before they cross the lines that require the foster system to become involved. Safe Families was founded in Chicago in 2003 and is primarily supported by the effort of volunteers. Today, the ministry has expanded to seventy cities in the United States, the United Kingdom, and Canada. The approach of Safe Families is to create an extended family support system for families going through a crisis. The extended family is made up of mostly Christ-following people who are trying to keep children safe and families together through mentoring relationships. Many factors contribute to families falling into crisis, including financial pressure, unemployment, domestic violence, and substance abuse. In these situations, churches and people of faith can partner with Safe Families to help for short periods of time to help when no one else can.[6]

Foster Parent Recruiting and Retention

The Compact Family Services organization offers resources and training to support foster families. Their web site is https://compact.family and https://agfostercare.network

Another quality organization called Promise686 provides training, resource manuals, and the steps needed to answer the question of how the church can support foster families. https://promise686.org

Adoptive Support - Project 1:27

Another resource churches can use is a Denver-based ministry called Project 1:27[7] to support the adoptive family when a child reaches this point in the process. In this ministry, adoptive families can receive care and support before and after the adoption process, making it more successful in the long run. They work directly with government agencies as well as foster and adoptive families. The ministry takes its name from James 1:27, where Jesus defines true religion as caring for the widows and the orphans. Project 1:27, along with the Colorado Department of Human Services, has helped lower the number of children waiting to be adopted from 800 to 365 in a two-year time frame.[8]

Foster Parent Support

Feedback from state and local officials about the current landscape of foster care indicated the need for someone to support foster parents because a support system of that kind did not currently exist in the social services sector. Therefore, I chose to evaluate a support system at Journey Church. My evaluation specifically focused on the satisfaction level of the support they received before and after the system was installed. Below is a description of the support system.

A foster parent support system is a framework for churches to use in providing care to foster families. This system is designed to train church leaders about the foster care problem and puts forth a plan for congregations that reduces the dropout rate of foster parents through practical levels of support.

Ted Stackpole is a U.S. missionary for the Assemblies of God working as a representative for Compact Services in Hot Springs, Arkansas. He provides training, support, and resources for churches interested in starting a foster care support program. Ted@ChaplainTed.US. Stackpole believes it is important for churches to start where they can and not lose momentum. The first step, according to him, is to recruit a family advocate who can do the job of matching up foster family needs with volunteers willing to support and serve them. He recommends one family advocate volunteer for every three to four foster families in the church. This will enable them to provide the focus they need to provide quality advocacy for each foster family. A natural place to look for these advocates is in the list of volunteers who sign up to help support foster families. Some may be equipped already to play the role of an advocate. He suggests asking for a one-year commitment to provide the consistency needed and establish relationships over a more extended period. This starting point for support puts a church in a strong position to focus on foster families with the greatest need. It also lowers the chance of these families dropping out. This will help keep the families at the highest risk of dropping out to stay in the game. The key, Stackpole says, is to "Start now and start supporting foster families because they have many more people in their lives than a typical family."[9] Once churches have volunteers and family advocates recruited, they can begin support group meetings for the foster families that have training and sharing opportunities at each gathering. Stackpole has seen these steps be successful at many other churches around the country and believes they are reproducible at any church in the country that wants to make a difference in foster care.

This support system seeks to address the problem of the lack of foster parent stability. From 1900 to 2000, the number of foster children in America grew from approximately 50,000 to 500,000. In 2017, that number rose to 660,000.[10] The same three problems that existed during the founding years of our nation still exists today:

1. Capacity: This is a problem today because there are not enough foster families for every foster child.
2. Stability: The families who foster are not adequately trained and supported
3. Quality: Children are not thriving in the current system

The government has attempted to solve this problem with state and county programs throughout the nation, but they are failing to meet the stated objectives. According to Compact Family Services research,

> An extensive three-year audit of state child welfare systems was conducted, and the Department of Health and Human Services found that not a single state

> complied with federal safety standards for children. Sixteen states did not meet any of these standards, and not a single state met more than two of the seven standards.[11]

To make matters worse, even the foster families recruited often drop out after the first year. About 40-60 percent of foster families drop out after the first year because of lack of support, training, paperwork requirements, court dates, calls, and numerous visits by officials.[12] This stability problem creates an environment that makes it even more difficult for the capacity issue. In fact, "The national average for a successful child placement after one year is only 34%."[13]

Compact Family Services believes that the church can be the solution. There are roughly 60,000,000 evangelicals in the United States and approximately 500,000 children in foster care today.[14] That's 120 evangelical Christians for every foster child in America. This means that there are more than enough evangelicals to meet the foster care need, and these evangelicals are required in James 1:27 to provide support because caring for the vulnerable is at the heart of the gospel.

The plan to address this need involves systematizing support. Each church can set out to recruit and support more foster families with more volunteers. Then the message becomes this: if someone decides to start fostering a child and attends a church providing support, they will not do it alone.

If someone decides to start fostering a child and attends a church providing support, they will not do it alone.

One volunteer is asked to be a family advocate who would take on the responsibility of matching up the needs of foster families with the skills and interests of the volunteers. This is a key role because this person becomes the go-to person for foster families. They need to anticipate the needs of foster families and make sure they are supported. Once the volunteers have been matched up, there is ongoing training for the volunteers to help them understand the trauma that foster children have and the type of support the foster families will require. The respite volunteers are scheduled with the families to give them a break and a time of rest.

Volunteers are asked to provide support in simple ways. For example, they might write a thank you note to a foster parent that encourages them and lets them know others want them to succeed. Email or text messages can be used as simple ways to reach out to the foster parent and offer to pray for them. Other volunteers might provide a gift card to a foster family or donate some well-needed supplies that the foster family usually must buy on their own. Volunteers can also offer the professional skills they have at a discounted or donated basis for foster families to show their support and help them care for the foster children in their homes for a more extended period. Examples of this might be free oil changes from a mechanic that attends the church or free lawncare by a landscaper that goes to the church and wants to help foster parents with what he or she does best. These are all simple ways everyone in the local church can do something to help children in need.

Each year a foster family support ministry will use the system so that new volunteers and foster families are recruited, and current foster families remain supported. In this way, churches will address the capacity, quality and sustainability issues in foster care and carry out their James 1:27 mandate to care for the orphans in their community.

Evaluating the Program

I sought to understand how impactful and effective the support model would be at Journey Church in retaining foster parents. Before we began, the dropout rate was 60 percent at Journey Church after one year without any support program. Dropout rate improvement was a key objective of my study and is a key objective for any church seeking to help provide stability for foster children.

Pre- and Post-Surveys

I planned to survey the foster families in the foster family support program before and after one year of implementation. The pre-study survey would create a baseline of data before the support program began, and then a post-study survey would provide data I could evaluate and use to analyze the overall support program's effectiveness and offer suggestions for improvement.

I also planned to evaluate the level of impact the support activities had on the overall satisfaction of each foster family to help reduce the dropout rate after one year.

Casting Vision and Setting Goals

Nationally, the number of foster parents available fails to meet the demand which is referred to as a capacity issue. Additionally, the foster care system continuously faces struggles with a low rate of retention known as a stability issue. Solving this need for capacity and stability in foster care seems to require a more comprehensive approach than is currently being offered.[15] Retention of foster families is an underlying issue I planned to explore because of the nationally high one-year dropout rate.[16] Dropout rates significantly contribute to the lack of available care for foster children and make it difficult for agencies to keep up with the demand for quality homes on a year-over-year basis.

In James 1:27, God commands the church of Jesus Christ to care for the widows and the orphans. This verse does not tell us how, nor does it say everyone should bring a child into his or her home, but it does say that every Christ follower should do something to help the most vulnerable children in their community. Therefore, I sought to understand how foster care connects to the heart of God and how more of God's people can participate.

I also expected that the leadership of Journey Church would gain a greater understanding as to its capacity to be more effective in caring for the orphans of Kenosha, Wisconsin. This congregation had in recent years become more aware of the foster care conversation and I believed had the potential to influence others at a local level with systems that found to be useful and effective. I felt convinced that church leaders and volunteers would gain greater spiritual insight into the heart of God to help foster children. Understanding God's heart in this way has the potential to help move any church forward as it more clearly understands the desire of her King. When churchgoers gain clarity about the biblical implications of caring for foster children and how that directly connects to their walk with God, they then question *how*. I knew that congregation attendees could practically live out the mission of God to the most vulnerable in their community and that both groups—church leaders and attendees—needed to know more deeply the biblical directives and practical ways to take more significant action so the church could display God's glory to the unbelievers by rescuing children in need.

During the time of launching this project at Journey Church in Kenosha, Wisconsin, I was serving in the role of an executive pastor. I regularly preached to the congregation, organized community outreach activities, and oversaw staff that led various ministries of the church. I had also developed several aspects of the foster care and adoption ministry by collaborating with staff to craft a vision in alignment with the overall direction of the church for this ministry.

As a result, in 2015, Journey Church leadership set a goal of helping 200 families become involved as a foster care or adoptive parent by the year 2020. A goal like this is significant because at the time there were 197 foster children in need of a home, and more would be added to that total by 2020. Two hundred foster families would ultimately meet the foster care need in Kenosha County and most likely create an excess of families from which workers could choose the best placement. A list like this had the potential to be a compelling reversal to a trend that was currently leaving children without anyone to care for them. Children without foster homes are placed in emergency care, relative care, or sent out of the county until a home can be located. When children are sent out of the county they are disconnected from friends, neighbors, and the school they attend. This removal is disruptive to their lives and adds to their trauma. A successful foster family support system can equip the church with a system of compassion to help meet the foster parent need and can strategically expand that church's impact into the local community with data that could influence other churches as well.

Journey Church started small with a few volunteers who had a heart for orphans, and over the years, it blossomed into a wave of momentum influencing twenty-six families to become foster and adoptive parents. Also, 35 percent of the pastoral staff at Journey Church in 2015 opened their homes to children in need as a result.

During this time of launching a foster care ministry at our church, I also founded a non-profit called 1Hope.community with the aim of rallying the churches in Kenosha around a few strategic issues like foster care. This organization came from the heart of our church's leadership with the desire to change the city by working together to offer hope.

Expecting Many Blessings

As I began to get more involved myself, I believed strongly that individuals and groups would strongly benefit from this ministry. Foster children would benefit as a result of increased recruitment and retention of foster parents over time. This would allow recruitment efforts from local agencies a legitimate chance to catch up with demand. In addition, the agencies would benefit because the support program could provide a first line of defense when foster families needed immediate help. Thus, case workers could be available to assist children in crisis instead of responding to needs that could be served by a local, well-trained volunteer. In this way, the agencies would be more successful at accomplishing their mission and meeting their goals for the community. I believed that the success of support care would also benefit the foster families because they would be cared for, appreciated, and encouraged to continue the effort they started by helping a child in need. Foster families would feel more fulfilled, equipped, encouraged, and more likely to recruit other foster parents themselves. The church would also benefit from a positive reputation because of successful support care.

Society has been searching for solutions to the gaps in foster parent support and has yet to offer a sustainable approach. God's glory is displayed as His church lives out James 1:27 and answers the call to help orphans by recruiting and retaining higher numbers of foster parents. Support volunteers are the key to meeting this need. These volunteers bless the community with their efforts but are also blessed personally as they experience spiritual growth from living a missional life in this way. Regardless of age, marital status, or church affiliation, adult volunteers that attend a local church doing support receive the opportunity to interact with foster families and realize that they play a part in extending the gospel to a vulnerable sector of the population. In this way, the volunteers become more understanding, and their compassion increases.

When watching a foster child being placed with a family for the first time, a lesson of compassion can be learned that only that experience can teach. A support care ministry can provide the opportunity for Christ-following volunteers to experience God in a way they otherwise would not experience.

The value of this research to the community is that once data are collected and used to demonstrate the effectiveness of support care in the local church, other churches can have a foundation for doing the same. One by one, community by community, churches can answer the call to help orphans, change futures, and impact entire communities.

Community Interviews

To further assist me in examining the need for a foster family support ministry at Journey Church, I contacted leaders of the foster care movement by phone to gain an understanding of what is working well and what needs still exist in the system that the church can address. These interviews helped create a focus on what aspects of foster care ministry Journey Church could employ to best carry out its biblical mandate to help the orphans in its city.

These interviews brought first-hand research credibility to the programmatic direction Journey Church chose in caring, supporting foster parents. Some of the targeted interviews included leaders at local adoption agencies, judges, and the district attorneys that work with cases every day. I interviewed state agencies and elected officials to discover the goals, laws, and issues important to them as well. I desired to gain clarity on the opinions of significant stakeholders in the Wisconsin child welfare system and to discover open doors for the church to display extravagant love to children and see God glorified.

State Representative Interview

Samantha Kerkman was a State Representative in the 61st District of Wisconsin and responded to an email request for updates about foster care legislation in the following manner: First, she pointed out that the State of Wisconsin formed a task force in 2017 to address the foster care need more effectively. According to the State Task Force website,

> Our bipartisan committee is tasked with developing ideas to improve the child welfare system. Our most recent numbers report that more than 7,000 children were placed in foster care in 2015. That is 300 more children than the previous year. If that trajectory

> continues, we could have 10,000 children in need of homes by 2023.[17]

This State website Kerkman referenced made several additional conclusions about the condition of foster care in Wisconsin that included a theory as to why the increase is occurring at such an alarming rate. They concluded, "The 71 counties other than Milwaukee had an increase of 6%. Nationally, the opioid epidemic is driving the increase in the number of children being taken out of their homes and placed in the foster care system."[18] They also found that "The two largest age groups in Out of Home Care are children aged 2-4, which accounts for 20% of all children in OHC and children aged 14-16, which account for 17.3% of all children in OHC."[19] The Task Force also discovered that 54.4 percent of the children in foster care in Wisconsin are Caucasian, 35.5 percent are African American, 7.3 percent are Native American, and 1.2 percent are Asian.[20]

Representative Kerkman also outlined the proposed legislative agenda in her email correspondence:[21] Of the thirteen legislative proposals, LRB 4925 and LRB 4929 are of particular interest because they propose funding for nonprofits that provide prevention solutions and care for the foster parents in the state. These proposals are proof of the need for supporting foster parents as a growing issue throughout Wisconsin.

Juvenile Court Judge Interview

On January 19, 2018, I asked Judge Jason Rossell to answer a few questions during a phone interview. Judge Rossell was responsible for making child welfare decisions for Kenosha County. My first question was: what critical elements of your work do you feel the local church needs to understand as they recruit foster families? He answered that biological families have complicated lives, and the children are going back to homes that are usually not as stable as their foster family. In his opinion, this is acceptable, because there is greater trauma done to the child if they are permanently removed from their biological family than if they stay with a more socioeconomically successful family in the community. His view is based on the belief that children continue to have an identity with their biological parents even after being placed with a foster family that is in a better socioeconomic situation.

Another example of this is how missions' trips from churches to foreign countries cannot fix the underlying causes of problems in a country. It is the same for a biological family because a preferable solution is not merely removing the children from their parents but helping the parents be better at parenting and living life. The issue of foster care is one of safety. Judge Rossell believes the church exists to be salt and light, but they may not be in a position to rescue every child. It is important not to judge the biological parent, he noted. A church congregation can do well to engage with the biological parent in a non-judgmental manner. Judge Rossell went on to say that integrating faith-based programs is not that hard in the judicial system and is often seamless. The challenge, however, is in organizing leaders that are not from the Department of Child and Family Services. This is where tensions can arise because contracts can be an issue."[22] The judge encouraged the church to support biological parents and the concept of reunification, emphasizing the desired win of seeing the child back with a stable biological parent as soon as possible.

When asked further about how the church could help specifically with the foster care crisis, the answer from the judge was especially interesting to Journey Church and the Assemblies of God, because he linked recruiting success with meeting the needs of the foster parents already involved. He stated that the church could help most by supporting the current foster parents in the system.

Social Service Supervisor Interview

I conducted an interview with Michelle Lang, a social services supervisor for Kenosha County, on March 2, 2018. During this phone interview, she thanked Journey Church for all it has done in the past few years to promote foster care in the congregation. According to Lang, Journey Church has been a force in the community and developed a strong pool of excellent foster parents who have made a real difference to hurting families. She went on to say that there is an ongoing need for further recruitment and that one of the best things the church can do for them is to make foster care visible and real by talking about it, promoting it, and doing it. Sometimes foster care seems invisible and suffers from lack of awareness, Lang added. Making it visible is a key to addressing the problem. When it comes to helping the Division of Health and Human Services the most, Lang said that fostering teens is the greatest need because there is a view that teens are harder to handle and therefore take much longer to get placed in a home. She also mentioned that other counties like Milwaukee have teen mentoring programs that have produced positive results.

When asked about the reasons people hesitate to serve as foster parents, she answered that the thought of the child returning home was a primary concern. Lang believes that people are usually not prepared mentally with the correct mindset that views foster care as a temporary solution leading to reunification. Reunification is why adults should get into foster parenting in the first place. Lang's final comments had to do with the need for biological parents to establish stronger relationships with the foster parents. She said, "When we see this happen, it makes for healthy progress in the parents' life and a smooth transition when reunification becomes a reality."[23]

District Attorney Interview

Michael Graveley is the District Attorney for Southeastern Wisconsin and has worked in that region for many years. He has experience with the judicial system and a working knowledge of how the community lives and moves on a daily basis. He understands the strengths and weaknesses of society. He knows who works together and who does not. He understands the political landscape and the dynamics of what it takes to see things change for the better.

When asked to describe how the foster system works and what improvements could be made, he offered this thought: "Foster families don't have control, and the District Attorney's office feels like the state needs to do a better job of sharing that big picture."[24] His point was that foster families could be empowered more effectively to understand the bigger context as it relates to the child they are caring for. Many times, there is behavior that could be managed better if the foster family was more informed about the background of the child. Not every detail can or should be disclosed, but according to the District Attorney, more information could be provided if state authorities agreed to do so. This improved context would also be helpful for foster families in understanding the relational dynamics that previously and currently exist. Many times, foster families are asked to interact with and even encourage the biological families without any understanding of the background, challenges or tendencies that exist. This information is currently not available to foster families but could serve as a powerful asset to trained foster families. Gravely says that

> Foster families help restore biological families because something has been profoundly broken. The first mission is to restore the broken family, and the second mission is to help the broken children thrive. Sometimes, those two missions are on the same path, but sometimes they feel like they go in opposite directions.[25]

This can be a tricky situation to navigate because sometimes the process stretches out for years, and the longer that timeframe is extended, the cloudier reunification goals can become. However, the District Attorney suggests a few steps that can be taken to improve the flow of information for foster families even in the current system:

1. The most effective method to increase awareness about the foster system, options, and the process is for foster families to support each other in dramatic ways. Graveley did not offer a specific way to create a support structure but suggested this would keep many more foster families in the game much longer and help them to be more effective.
2. The foster care system can be scary and intimidating. It is important to find people that can be known and trusted by the foster parents. Therefore, the District Attorney suggested calling his office and asking questions, because the more people learn, the more equipped and confident they are to advocate for a child that needs care.
3. Advocacy in legislation is another powerful way a foster family can make a difference and improve the system. Graveley suggests that privacy legislation may need to change to allow foster parents to gain a bigger picture. State representatives like Samantha Kerkman and Peter Barka would have an open ear to this issue. Social services and the District Attorney work together to introduce bills for consideration each year and work with the Madison Association that advocates for children's rights.

When asked about how the local church can help the District Attorney's office, the topic of recruitment was front and center. There is a need for more foster families in the city of Kenosha as well as the State of Wisconsin. According to the Social Services of Kenosha County at the time of this interview, the number of children in the foster care system increased 18 percent in 2016, and on any given day there are 132 children in the Kenosha County system. Churches can help with this effort by partnering together. Graveley believes that Journey Church is a church that has a true mission in the community for change. He also believes Journey is a living example of what a positive clear vision can do. He values foster care personally as an eight on a scale of one to ten and feels a city is judged by how it cares for the most vulnerable.

When asked about the strategic nature of placing children into the homes of families instead of using a group home model, Graveley responded by recalling the movement in our country to close orphanage group homes in the 1960s and 1970s. He said that when children are placed in a safe home, they receive the care and attention needed to heal and thrive. Graveley felt that foster parents are true heroes, and he was passionate about that point. He went on to say, "The world is full of people that will talk a good game, but it is foster parents truly that walk the walk."[26]

Group Interview with Social Services

My wife Wendy was a foster parent in Kenosha County who became a catalyst for a focus group listening session with foster parents on September 13, 2017. This focus group was to be a platform to share suggestions with social services leadership. The meeting was organized to learn more about what can be done to support foster families more effectively with the input of twenty-five people present who represented foster families in the county.

The results were amazing! Many wonderful ideas came from this collaborative meeting and were implemented within a very short time. New follow up procedures, additional appreciation, and even a new program for recruiting more foster parents was discussed and eventually implemented. Many of the ideas that came from this one collaborative meeting have had years of positive impact on the effort of supporting foster parents in the county.

This meeting also demonstrated how one person can make a difference by simply talking to leadership about possible enhancements to the current system. This conversation was filled with hope because the foster care county leadership was very supportive and open to ideas that would help the children they serve. Everyone made a difference together.

Each interview described how churches can help most with foster care by recruiting and retaining foster parents. Support for foster families was expressed as the area of need that was not currently be addressed and was strongly needed.

Be encouraged that one person like you can facilitate a listening session with foster parents and community leadership. You can be a catalyst for positive change by getting involved.

CHAPTER 14

Local Church Pilot: Evaluation

Discovered Outcomes

My study observed important connections between the effectiveness of the foster parent support ministry at Journey Church and its value in the practical theology of orphan care. Faith is lived out in practical ways, and God uses many different people to work together for his purposes and his glory. My research sought to not only shed light on what the secular world was attempting to do for foster children but also how the faith community is currently deploying resources and strategies to address the same need. The beauty of a study like this is that it seeks to find authentic ways the church can help the unchurched world accomplish something they have not been able to do by themselves up to this point. It may be a new day for the church if state and local leaders begin to not only listen but also work with the church to care for the forgotten in their communities.

Success in this area by Journey Church will be far-reaching in scope because of the influence this church has within various communities. First, the successful implementation of foster care support ministry served as a feeder to the adoption and foster care efforts the church already had put forth. Those children needing permanency would finally find it with more Christian families responding to the need. A new wave, however, emerged, because as Journey Church discovered effective ministry to foster children, other churches saw how they too could make a difference with their congregations. When churches work together in this way, the need for foster homes can be met, and the door will open for other churches to follow suit. Church leaders in every state can follow this blueprint of ministry and develop their custom plan to carry out true religion themselves. Historically, the church has responded to children in need over the centuries in different ways, but this study identified how the culture and faith community could support foster care today.

Evaluating the Survey Data

To help evaluate the satisfaction level of the Journey Church foster parent support ministry, I first used a qualitative survey method to create a baseline of satisfaction that could be used for comparison after the ministry was in place. My hypothesis was that when additional care and support were applied to existing foster parents, their levels of satisfaction and retention would increase. I designed this survey to determine if my underlying assumption was correct and if so, to what extent. I also wanted the survey to identify specific areas of support that foster parents most appreciated and found helpful.

Developing a Database of Foster Parents

To create a foster parent support ministry, I first needed to create a database of active foster parents at Journey Church. I sent out a church-wide survey to 2,500 people to populate a database and understand the landscape of foster care activity in the congregation. Of the total possible respondents, 7 percent (or 183 people) responded to the survey. The survey thus informed the church of how many people were involved in foster care, adoption, and respite care. After completing this survey, I discovered several relevant data points:

1. One hundred fifty-five of the 183 respondents provided their phone number for future contact.
2. One hundred percent of respondents provided their email address.
3. Seventy-nine percent of respondents have considered involvement in foster care or adoption.
4. Thirty percent of respondents have been foster or adoptive parent in the past or present.
5. Eighty-three percent of respondents would be interested in foster parent support groups.
6. Forty families have become involved in foster care or adoption the last five years while 143 have considered involvement during that time

Pre- and Post-Study Survey Development

With a database of active foster families created, new survey questions were formulated to learn more about the possible value of a support foster parent ministry. This new pre- and post-study survey became the focus of this project study.

The questions utilized in this survey were taken from a previous research instrument designed by Bill Hancock who founded FaithBridge Foster Care in Alpharetta, Georgia. During a phone interview, Mr. Hancock provided the framework for this research apparatus as it was used previously.[1] FaithBridge is a professionally managed foster care agency that used these same questions to assess the satisfaction level of foster parents they served on an annual basis.

I used a SurveyMonkey survey for data collection because of its ability to quickly distribute, collect, and tabulate results for the researcher. I then exported data from this software. SurveyMonkey provided summary information as well as comprehensive breakdowns of reported results, percentages, and independent comments from respondents.

At the time of the survey, all respondents were attendees of Journey Church and served as active foster parents licensed with a local agency in Kenosha, Wisconsin. The foster parents were adults who have all participated in state training to serve as foster parents in Wisconsin. Detailed demographics of the respondents were not determined relevant to my desired outcomes and therefore were not collected.

The first question was posed to authenticate that each respondent was an active foster parent at Journey Church. The second question was meant to create a baseline satisfaction level for the overall foster care ministry before the support program was implemented. The next two open-ended questions were asked to capture support method suggestions that the researcher may not have been aware of. This was followed by several questions that addressed the popular support areas of respite, babysitting, and transportation as identified by the FaithBridge Foster Care agency professionals. The survey ended with several questions about the top support needs, professional agency satisfaction, and the likelihood of retention in the upcoming year.

In total, I designed fourteen questions to take under seven minutes to answer, wording them in a conversational tone to help facilitate high comprehension. I sent out an email to all respondents, including a link to the survey and a paragraph explaining the purpose of the survey and the benefits that could be gained from the data generated by their invested time.

Pre-Study Survey Results

The Journey Church foster parent support pre-study survey was administered in October before the ministry began its operation on January 1. This pre-study survey was sent out to twenty-seven active foster parents in the church to create a baseline for further comparison; fourteen surveys were completed, representing a >50 percent response rate.

Of the fourteen respondents, a variety of interesting results were identified from this baseline research. First, it was noteworthy that without a formal program in place, 0 percent of the respondents ranked the effectiveness of church support at the highest level of a five on a 0-5 scale. Seventy-nine percent of respondents ranked church support of foster parents a 3 or lower. This, however, would seem appropriate at this stage of foster parent support because there was no formal program in place. The fact that some level of support was perceived among most respondents was encouraging.

Within this control group of fourteen foster parents, 14 percent reported having no likelihood of returning when asked about their intent to continue being a foster parent into the next year, and 36 percent reported having decided or were considering the end of their service in the next year. This rate is very close to the 40-60 percent national drop-out rate for foster parents after one year and signaled to me a need for help with retention among the foster parents at Journey Church.[2] (As noted earlier, the goal of the support system is to significantly lower this drop-out rate with a systemized support program in the local church.)

Despite the ranking of needs, there was a small half-point variance between the top four needs (3.0 – 3.6 average score) of babysitting, family mentoring, respite, and transportation. All four were high on the list of responses. These questions were assessed with a weighted score in a matrix question on the survey that used a 1-5 scale from least to greatest for each category. This survey was re-issued to the same control group just over one year later to determine what effect the foster parent support ministry had on this group.

Launching the Program

I conducted training during the first half of 2018. Volunteers were recruited and completed phase one of the support training. These training steps and motivational events continued for six months for the fifty recruited volunteers and included trauma-informed care, leadership training, and program-specific training. Not all the volunteers, however, completed the required training, which left a pool of thirty-three support volunteers ready to engage in this ministry.

In August of 2018, the foster parent support ministry officially began as the first of its kind at Journey Church. To those who had benefited from the newly formed foster parent support ministry, the satisfaction survey was re-issued after one year of activity.

In the same way, these nine foster parents attended Journey Church at the time of the survey and were licensed by the state for foster care with a child placed in their home. It was interesting to note that the church did not do a foster parent recruiting push in 2018, which means the data was not infused with many new, optimistic foster parents. This control group had been serving for over a year with only a few new foster parents added to the group during that time.

Pre- and Post-Study Comparison

After comparing the satisfaction rates of foster parents before and after receiving support care, the foster family support system improved the overall satisfaction of being a foster parent by 25%! This is an important and felt change because it demonstrates with real data, how support does encourage those answering the call to care for children in need. In addition, this encouragement also lowered the dropout rate of foster families. These two factors play a key role in the effective retention of more foster families.

Greatest Support Needed

Babysitting was listed as the greatest need in both pre- and post-study surveys. The score for babysitting ranked higher in the post-study survey than it had ranked earlier. The average score for babysitting in the pre-study survey was 3.60 and increased to 4.14 in the post-study survey. It is unclear as to exactly why this increased in perceived value, but we do know from the data that more foster parents received babysitting once the program began than they did before. Of the respondents, 56 percent reported receiving babysitting support in the previous thirty days after the program was installed compared to only 7.1 percent in the pre-study survey. One possibility is that since more people experienced the value of having babysitting support, they ranked it higher on the list of perceived needs. This area of support appears to be the single greatest area of improvement for the ministry in one year.

While babysitting was identified as the greatest need on both surveys, encouraging notes and supplies took the number two and three spots for greatest needs identified after the program was installed. The one significant outlier was marriage mentoring because it dropped from the number two overall perceived need in the pre-study survey all the way to last place in the post-study survey. Again, it is not clear why this was the case, but further follow-up could be done to gain a deeper understanding. One possibility for why encouraging notes, meals, and supplies may have moved so far up the rankings of perceived needs is because these services were being provided regularly by the ministry. Therefore, once the respondents received these support resources, they valued them much higher than before. If this is true, then the study may be reflecting a relationship that exists between services provided by support care and the perceived value of those services by the foster parents.

Likelihood to Continue

The pre-study survey reported 14 percent of foster parents saying there was zero chance they would continue being a foster parent in the upcoming year. After program implementation, however, that percentage dropped to **zero** among survey respondents! Stated another way, *none of the foster parents said they would be dropping out in* *the upcoming year after the program was installed.* This result would seem to be a measured victory for the efforts of support care ministry at Journey Church because all the active foster parents who responded to the survey reported that there was some level of likelihood they would continue in that capacity into the next year.

Contribution to the Ministry

Overall, the results of the pre- and post-study survey were informative in many ways. The ministry leadership could see that foster family support had a positive impact on retention levels and ministry satisfaction levels after only a relatively short time of providing support. This short-term impact offers hope that with more time, training, and evaluation the ministry has room to improve its satisfaction levels even more significantly. Journey Church leaders also could see the areas of strength such as babysitting, encouraging notes, meals, and proving supplies.

See Appendix A: Church Survey.

CONCLUSION

Throughout history, there have always been children who have tragically found themselves without parents to care for them. Each culture has addressed this need in a variety of ways. Today, we wrestle specifically with how to serve the approximately 500,000 children in the United States who are in this situation.[1] Foster Children are a high-risk population who are often victims of human trafficking if permanent homes are not found. [2] Therefore, since foster children are a vulnerable segment of the population, and since Scripture clearly admonishes Christ followers to serve and love the marginalized to demonstrate God's love to a hurting world, helping these children is at the heart of the gospel.

God has used and wants to continue to use the church as an agent of rescue for these vulnerable children in society. When the church obeyed the Word of God and helped the fatherless children, the world took notice. Similarly, today, the church is on mission when it cares for the most vulnerable children of our communities.

A church does not know its Master if it does not care for the poor and the vulnerable. Empowered by the Spirit, the Church must take action in this direction and care for the widows and orphans of our time.

We see God redefining the family by placing a higher value on spiritual connection with God rather than earthly bloodlines. The mere fact that God allows all people to be made one with Him through a spiritual adoption process sets the stage for Christians to be that same gospel to broken children by opening their homes for a season or for a lifetime. Christian foster families are Jesus to foster children because they are an extension of what Jesus has done for each believer. This is an opportunity the Church has in order to influence the culture today through love.

Society has also attempted throughout history to find solutions for orphaned children. The results, however, have produced mixed reviews. Today there is a new approach called support ministry that offers hope to foster care in every county and every state through a church-based foster family support system. This program organizes support care for foster parents that shows them what they are doing matters to the church and to the heart of God. There is now an opportunity for the church to provide a way for all Christians to obey James 1:27 and serve orphans with collective impact like the early church had in Acts chapter 2. Furthermore, there is an opportunity today for the church to show the world that it knows its Master by caring for the poor and broken children of our day. The foster family support system is designed to take advantage of these opportunities and position the Church as the global leader God intended for it to be.

This local church-based program was the focus of a pilot study I conducted as part of my doctoral studies. This study set out to understand more about the practical theology of foster care ministry and to evaluate the satisfaction of the Journey Church support ministry in Kenosha, Wisconsin, in particular. I established three goals for this study, and the following are conclusions drawn from each goal.

Goal 1 - Biblical Mandate

Vulnerable children need to be cared for by the church. Children in foster care are a marginalized population in need of being saved. They need a voice. In Luke 4:17-21 when He is beginning His ministry, Jesus declares that He has come for that very mission. When the church aligns itself with the mission of Christ and meets the needs of these poor children, the prophetic words of Jesus become a reality. Children are saved because Jesus came to earth, died, and began the Church through his Holy Spirit. There is an excellent purpose in foster care ministry because it was the mission of Christ to redeem creation, and that includes "The removal of the word orphan from the human vocabulary."[3]

Rescuing hurt and broken people aligns with the character of God, and we see this in the biblical text when the church was instructed by the prophet Isaiah and the Apostle Paul with powerful language. James was also vocal about the connection between compassion and the gospel, because helping others in need remains critical to the mission of Christ. When the church loves vulnerable children, the world sees the power that God has to change the lives of people forever through His beautiful love.

Therefore, there is a right way and a wrong way for the church to go in the eyes of God. This issue is not gray in the Book of Isaiah but rather clear in Isaiah's directive. The right way leads to blessing and is presented in Isaiah 1:16-17, when Israel is called to repent and display God's glory by caring for the oppressed.[4] The wrong way leads to separation from God when His people seek favor with offerings and rituals instead of helping the most vulnerable in society.

God tells His people through Isaiah clearly and boldly that neglecting the poor and vulnerable is not acceptable. Israel's neglect proved they no longer knew the Lord (Isa 1:3). Isaiah strongly states that the Israelites had been reduced to a level even lower than animal status because even the ox knows its master. This wrong way of behaving as God's people would end in disaster if not corrected.[5]

God cares so much for the poor and vulnerable that when He had an opportunity to direct the way that the church would display justice, He chose widows and orphans as the focus of His compassion because they were the most vulnerable in society. Isaiah spoke in a way that offered hope for a better tomorrow when the people of God met this need. Our mandate today is no less compelling.

Luke highlights the power of serving others in his teachings as he spends considerable time speaking about the poor. He describes how the hearts of people are more open to the gospel after they are shown compassion and love. Serving those who are different from us demonstrates the love Jesus exemplified. This is the way God expects the church to function today.

The promise at Pentecost (Acts 2) was for every believer, every member of the family, and every class of citizen. It was an event that brought equality to all people to share the gospel. This account stands at the heart of the New Testament, because at that point the Holy Spirit forms the Church. Luke's writings in his Gospel and in Acts focus on the mission of Christ to set the captives free. Therefore, if Luke's writings were at the heart of the New Testament, and he indeed focuses on the marginalized, then one can conclude that serving the vulnerable children in our society is at the heart of the gospel.

When the church serves those in need as it did in Acts 6, it puts the gospel into action, thus connecting those actions to a commanded blessing from God. The Acts 6 storyline of the Spirit follows those who were doing what Christ had asked the church to do in serving the poor. Therefore, the church today has the same potential to effect change as the Early Church did because the same Holy Spirit empowers it with the same calling.

Additionally, the book of James brings clarity about the value of the poor.[6] Helping the poor is an expression of a life lived for Christ and is what makes a Christian community like the Church authentic in its claims. When the mandate in James 1:27 is lived out before the world because of faith in Christ, a powerful message of love is sent that brings glory to God.[7] It is a message of love, and love is the thesis of God's Word.

Paul's writings also clarify what God requires of His people; as well, they inform God's people what He has available for them to carry out His commands. He teaches that God's mechanism for a restored relationship with Him is spiritual adoption through Jesus Christ.[8] In the same way we are accepted and adopted into the kingdom of God through Christ, a child can be accepted and made part of a new earthly family through the adoption process. It is because the Church has been adopted into the kingdom of God that they may be compelled to extend the gospel in the same way to a child through foster care or adoption. Both are done in love and come with the promise of an inheritance.[9]

In the same way we are accepted and adopted into the kingdom of God through Christ, a child can be accepted and made part of a new earthly family through the adoption process.

The spirit of adoption is not only the way each person arrives in heaven, but it is also the Christian mission in life to love those in need.[10] Even if there is a cost to helping the fatherless and marginalized, the local church can serve freely, knowing that they already have all the riches in heaven they could ever want waiting for them in the future.[11] Consequently, as the church becomes more aware of the spirit of adoption, they begin to understand the gospel more richly.[12]

Goal 2 - Greater Perspective through a Historical and Church Approach

The Hebrew culture of the Old Testament would look to the extended family to care for a child who did not have parents in their life. Families mainly viewed the function of a child at that time as survival.[13] Gender determined economic value, and children were abandoned to control the impact of the family inheritance.[14] This was a cultural norm in Greek culture as well, and it continued into the first century. Finally, after Pentecost, the church became vocal about the equality of human life and stood up to care for abandoned children. This stance eventually impacted culture and made the abandonment of children illegal for the first time. It is reasonable to conclude that Pentecost resulted in the rescue of vulnerable infants for generations to come. In this way, the church changed the culture by working together on a cause they knew broke the heart of God.

The New Testament Church has impacted the way the world helps poor children. It has done this by adopting abandoned infants, establishing orphanages, conceiving innovative outplacement solutions like the orphan train at the turn of the twentieth century, and championing global adoption campaigns. These efforts and countless others have revolutionized the world's approach to addressing the orphan crisis throughout history.

Today, however, only 12 percent of Protestant churches report having talked about foster care or adoption over the past twelve months. On this issue the church has been increasingly inactive despite the strong missional connection of foster care and adoption to the heart of the gospel. When the other 88 percent of churches get involved, the potential to reverse many devastating trends will be enormous. For example, every foster child reunified or adopted is one where human trafficking, homelessness, incarceration, substance abuse, and/or teen pregnancy is prevented. The New Testament Church has a history of leading the way in helping vulnerable children and is positioned to rise together once again. The church is the solution to the foster care crisis in America, and the model of support care provides a strategy for advocacy, service projects, recruitment, and volunteer management so that everyone can do something.

Goal 3 - Evaluation of Foster Family Support Ministry

The local church and foster care agencies in America both have something in common: they both care about helping vulnerable children. Agencies have the systems and churches have the people. Therefore, together, they have the potential to meet the growing needs of foster families in America. The main reason the local church is positioned to be the answer to the capacity and stability problem in foster care is that helping vulnerable children is in alignment with its mission and the character of God.

A foster family support system aims to empower the local church to take action against the lack of capacity and stability among foster parents nationwide. Journey Church in Kenosha, Wisconsin used this system with positive results after twelve months of implementation and experienced a positive shift in overall satisfaction of the foster care ministry by 25 percent. There was also a 14 percent reduction in the number of foster parents who were determined to drop out in the following year.

The surveys showed babysitting was the greatest need, followed by encouraging notes and supplies.

The surveys showed babysitting was the greatest need, followed by encouraging notes and supplies.

I observed several key implications from this study. The first is that the support program was found to have a positive impact on the stability of foster parents who attend a church with this ministry. Other churches may be able to expect similar results when applying the same system in their congregation. For example, a smaller congregation than Journey Church could expect increased retention levels of foster parents but may only have two foster families active in their church. The results, in this case, maybe similar overall, but the ratios will likely adjust to fit the size of each church.

Provided that this support ministry increases capacity and retention rates of foster parents, it has an opportunity to be one of the ways everyone in a local church can do something to help orphaned children. The project could also have state and national implications, because foster care agencies report numbers back to the state. This possibility means that when churches work together using a support system, the likelihood of meeting foster care needs by the body of Christ go up dramatically. This outcome would likely draw attention from other counties in the state as well as from statewide administration.

Personal Reflection

My doctoral research on foster care and adoption and the subsequent implementation of a one-year support system at Journey Church impacted me both professionally and personally. As a pastor, this project provided me with both a theological and practical framework from which to address various types of needs in our community in the future. The application of this study was targeted to foster care ministry, but the heart of God for the poor and vulnerable applies in many different settings. My theological study opened my eyes to how strongly God expects the church to serve those in need. I knew that serving was important for the church, but now I see it as *mission critical* to the identity of Christ followers. The world should know that the church is committed to helping those in need. It should be our brand, our tagline.

Professionally, the process of connecting with local, state, and national leaders about the needs of foster care ministry energized me when I became aware of the universal need for foster parent support. It was stated as a gap in the system by everyone I spoke to at every level. Therefore, the chance to meet that need with the support system was exhilarating and fueled this project from start to finish.

Personally, this project changed the trajectory of my life. In the time it took to complete this study, I fostered and adopted three children. Currently, I have six children and can testify that opening our home to the community through foster care has taught everyone in our family more about the gospel than we have ever known before. My older children serve God and their community every day by helping to love our adopted children. As parents, we see the reward in the sacrifices made for our now adopted children in the way they have grown and developed over the years.

I have also been reinvigorated by the future power potential of the church. This study has shown me how the New Testament Church led the way in the Church serving those in need throughout the generations. It was amazing to comprehend that the words of the Bible have power because when children were set out to die in the first century, they were rescued by Christ-following adults. It was also fascinating to learn how the Catholic Church was so committed to making a safe place for the orphans who lived in America during its early years as a nation. These examples inspired me about what the Church in America can do in the future when it works together on an issue so close to God's heart. Together, as Christ's love compels us, we can reach out in compassionate care through actions motivated by the gospel, showing a skeptical world who God is. We can love because He first loved us.

APPENDIX A

1. Are You currently a foster Parent? Yes or No
2. Based on providing you with volunteer support services, how would you rate the current effectiveness of our foster care and adoptive ministry?

    0=poor 5=Excellent
3. As a foster parent, what do you need to feel supported by your friends and local church family?
4. What are your CORE needs as a foster family?
5. Have you had access to babysitting from a church volunteer in the last 30 days?
6. If yes: How would you rate the quality of baby sitting on a scale of 0-5.
7. Have you received respite (overnight childcare) support from a church volunteer in the last 30-60 days?
8. If yes, how would you rate the quality of respite (overnight childcare) on a scale of 0-5.
9. Have you received transportation support from a volunteer in the last 30 days?
10. If yes how would you rate the quality of the transportation support? 0-5 scale?
11. How supported do you feel from the case worker agency? 0-5 scale
12. How likely are you to continue being a foster parent in the next year? Scale of 0-5.

13. Please rank the following support services based on your greatest need:
    1. Baby sitting
    2. Transportation
    3. Respite (Overnight Childcare)
    4. Meals and supplies
    5. Encouraging Notes
    6. Marriage and family mentoring/counseling

SELECT RESOURCES

"The AFCARS Report." *US Department of Health and Human Services* 23 (June 2016): 6. www.acf.hhs.gov/programs/cb.

Bakke, Odd Magne. *When Children Became People: The Birth of Childhood in Early Christianity*. Minneapolis, MN: Fortress Press, 2005.

Barnhill, Carla. "Churches Adopt Adoption: Project 1:27." *ChristianityToday.Com*. Accessed November 24, 2016. http://www.christianitytoday.com/ct/2010/july/11.23.html.

Bigger, Stephen. "The Exposure of Infants among Jews and Christian in Antiquity." *Journal for the Study of the Old Testament* 35, no. 5 (June 2011): 66-66. Accessed May 22, 2017.

Bowley, Mary Frances, and Jennifer Bradley Franklin. *Make It Zero: The Movement to Safeguard Every Child*. Chicago, IL: Moody Publishers, 2016.

Brewer, Samantha R. "Wealth and Poverty in Luke's Gospel and Acts: A Challenge to the Christian Church." *Encounter: Journal for Pentecostal Ministry* 6 (2009): 4.

"Children Aging Out of Foster Care." *New Jersey Child Placement Advisory Council*, 2016. Accessed July 23, 2017. http://www.njcpac.org/aging-out/.

Cruver, Dan. "Adoption Is Bigger than You Think." *The Journal of Discipleship & Family Ministry* 4, no. 1 (September 2013): 72-73. Accessed November 2, 2016. http://www.sbts.edu/family/2014/04/16/equipping-the-generations-adoption-is-bigger-than-you-think/

D'Amico, Jean, Kelvin Pollard, and Alicia VanOrman. *2018 Kids Count Data Book: State Trends in Child Well-Being*. Baltimore, MD: Annie E. Casey

Foundation, 2018. Accessed October 21, 2018, https://www.aecf.org/resources/2018-kids-count-data-book/

Deymaz, Mark. *Disruption: Repurposing The Church To Redeem The Community.* Nashville, TN: Thomas Nelson, 2017.

Forbes, Heather, and B. Bryan Post. *Beyond Consequences, Logic, and Control: A Love Based Approach to Helping Children with Severe Behaviors.* 2nd ed. Boulder, CO: Beyond Consequences Institute, LLC, 2009.

House, Paul R. "Isaiah's Call and Its Context in Isaiah 1-6." *Criswell Theological Review,* no. 6.2 (1993): 207-222.

Moore, Russell D. *Adopted for Life: The Priority of Adoption for Christian Families & Churches.* Wheaton, IL: Crossway Books, 2009.

National Foster Care and Family Restoration Ministry Model. Hot Springs, AR: AGFSA and FaithBridge Foster Care, February 2013.

Post, Neil. *The Disappearance of Childhood.* New York: Vintage Books, Random House, 1994.

Purvis, Karyn B., David R. Cross, and Wendy Lyons Sunshine. *The Connected Child: Bring Hope and Healing to Your Adoptive Family.* New York: McGraw-Hill Publishers, 2007. Kindle.

Rodriguez, Dario Lopez. *The Liberating Mission of Jesus: The Message of the Gospel of Luke.* Eugene, OR: Pickwick Publications, 2012.

Schooler, Jane E., Betsy Keefer Smalley, and Timothy J. Callahan. *Wounded Children Healing Homes: How Traumatized Children Impact Adoptive and Foster Families.* Colorado Springs, CO: Nav Press, 2009.

Swinton, John, and Brian Brock. *A Graceful Embrace: Theological Reflections on Adopting Children.* Vol. 4. Boston, MA: Brill, 2018.

Westerlund, Katarina. "Adoption as Spiritual Praxis in Individualized Times." *Dialog* 51, no. 4 (2012): 323-329. Accessed November 2, 2016. https://onlinelibrary-wiley-com.seu.idm.oclc.org/journal/15406385.

ENDNOTES

Preface

1 Results of evaluative tools indicated that Journey Church used this system with positive results after twelve months of implementation and experienced a positive shift in overall satisfaction of the foster care ministry by 25 percent. In addition, the number of foster parents who were determined to drop out in the upcoming year was reduced from 14 percent to 0 percent after support methods were applied. These two data points suggest that local churches can positively impact stability and retention levels of foster parents through the CompaCare System of Compassion.

PART TWO

1 Bill Hancock and Johan Mostert, *CompaCare Compassion Care System Manual: Helping Churches Minister to Vulnerable Children and Families* (Hot Springs, AR: Compact Family Service, 2017), 39.
2 Elizabeth Achtemeier, "Plumbing the Riches: Deuteronomy for the Preacher," *Interpretation* 41, no. 3 (1987): 271, accessed November 30, 2016, http://int.sagepub.com/content/41/3/269.short.
3 Ibid.
4 Ibid.

Chapter 6: Compassion for Orphans

1 Karyn B. Purvis, David R. Cross, and Wendy Lyons Sunshine, *The Connected Child: Bring Hope and Healing to Your Adoptive Family* (New York: McGraw-Hill Publishers, 2007), loc 269, Kindle.
2 Ibid., loc 265.
3 Ibid., loc 273.
4 Ibid., loc 250.

5 Hancock and Mostert, *CompaCare Compassion Care System Manual*, 32.
6 Ibid., 33.
7 Annie E. Casey Foundation, "Child Welfare and Foster Care Statistics," Last updated September 26, 2022, accessed April 3, 2023, https://www.aecf.org/blog/child-welfare-and-foster-care-statistics.
8 "Children Aging out of Foster Care," *New Jersey Child Placement Advisory Council*, 2016, accessed July 23, 2017, http://www.njcpac.org/aging-out/.
9 Paul R. House, "Isaiah's Call and its Context in Isaiah 1-6," *Criswell Theological Review* 6, no. 2 (1993): 207.
10 Gregory Goswell, "Isaiah 1:26: A Neglected Text on Kingship," *Tyndale Bulletin* 62, no. 2 (2011): 236.
11 House, "Isaiah's Call," 208.
12 John N. Oswalt, *The NIV Application Commentary: Isaiah* (Grand Rapids, MI: Zondervan Publishing House, 2003), 77.
13 Ibid., 78.
14 Ibid.
15 Ibid., 80.
16 Karl N. Jacobson and Rolf A. Jacobson, "The One Who Will Be Born: Preaching Isaiah's Promises in a Harry Potter Culture," *Word and World* 27, no. 4 (2007): 427.
17 R. Laird Harris, Gleason L. Archer, and Bruce K. Waltke, *Theological Wordbook of the Old Testament* (Chicago, IL: Moody Publishers, 1999), 863.
18 C. Hassell Bullock, *An Introduction to The Old Testament Prophetic Books*, updated ed. (Chicago, IL: Moody Publishers, 2007), 161.
19 Rolf A. Jacobson, "The Lord is a God of Justice: The Prophetic Insistence on Justice in Social Context," *Word and World* 30, no. 2 (2010): 126.
20 Ibid.
21 Ibid.
22 Ibid., 128.
23 Susan Niditch, *The Composition of Isaiah* (Amherst, MA: Amherst College, Department of Religion, n.d.), 509.
24 Ibid.
25 Marvin A. Sweeney, Carol A. Dempsey, and Gale A. Yee, *The Prophets: Isaiah 1-39*, study ed. (Minneapolis, MN: Augsburg Fortress, 2016), 676.

Chapter 7: Empowerment to Care for Orphans

1 Robert Jamieson, A. R. Fausset, and David Brown, *Commentary Critical and Explanatory on the Whole Bible* (Oak Harbor, WA: Logos Research Systems, Inc., 1997), 173.

2 John D. Barry et al., *Faithlife Study Bible* (Bellingham, WA: Lexham Press, 2012), n.p.
3 David Dockery, *Holman Concise Bible Commentary* (Nashville, TN: Broadman and Holman Publishers, 1998), 507.
4 Carol A. Newsom, Sharon H. Ringe, and Jacqueline Lapsley, *Women's Bible Commentary*, rev. ed. (Louisville, KY: Westminster John Knox Press, 2012), 537.
5 Ajith Fernando, *The NIV Application Commentary: Acts* (Grand Rapids, MI: Zondervan, 1998), 228
6 Merrill C. Tenney, *New Testament Survey* (Grand Rapids, MI: Wm. B. Eerdmans Publishing Company, 1985), 241.
7 Fernando, *NIV Application Commentary: Acts*, 225.
8 Ibid.
9 Ibid., 226.
10 Ibid., 227.
11 Stanley M. Horton, *The Book of Acts: The Wind of the Spirit* (Springfield, MO: Gospel Publishing House, 1996), 84.
12 Stanley M. Horton, *What The Bible Says About The Holy Spirit* (Springfield, MO: Gospel Publishing House, 1995), 152.
13 Stanley M. Horton, *Acts: A Logion Press Commentary* (Springfield, MO: Logion Press, 2012), 136.
14 Ted Cabal et al., *The Apologetics Study Bible: Real Questions, Straight Answers, Strong Faith* (Nashville, TN: Holman Bible Publishers, 2007), n.p.
15 Andrew Knowles, *The Bible Guide*, vol. 1 (Minneapolis, MN: Augsburg Books, 2001), 543.
16 Samantha R. Brewer "Wealth and Poverty in Luke's Gospel and Acts: A Challenge to the Christian Church," *Encounter: Journal for Pentecostal Ministry* 6 (2009): 4.
17 Dario Lopez Rodriguez, *The Liberating Mission of Jesus: The Message of the Gospel of Luke* (Eugene, OR: Pickwick Publications, 2012), 26.

Chapter 8: Equity for the Poor

1 LeAnn Snow Flesher, "Mercy Triumphs over Judgment: James as Social Gospel," *Review & Expositor* 111, no. 2 (2014): 183.
2 Mariam Kamell, "James 1-27 and the Church's Call to Mission and Morals," *CRUX* 46, no. 4 (2010): 18.
3 Flesher, "Mercy Triumphs," 183.
4 Kamell, "James 1-27," 16.
5 Ibid., 17.

6 Toby Ziglar, "When Words Get in the Way of True Religion James 1: 19-27," *Review & Expositor* 100 (2003): 274.
7 James L. Boyce, "A Mirror of Identity: Implanted Word and Pure Religion in James 1:17-27," *Word and World* 35, no. 3 (2015): 213.
8 Kamell, "James 1-27," 21.
9 Joseph Allen, "Renewal of the Christian Community: A Challenge for Pastoral Ministry," *St. Vladimir's Theological Quarterly* 29, no. 4 (1985): 305.

Chapter 9: The Spirit of Adoption

1 Walter Brueggemann, *The Prophetic Imagination*, 2nd ed. (Nashville: Fortress Press, 2001), 33.
2 John Swinton and Brian Brock, *A Graceful Embrace: Theological Reflections on Adopting Children*, vol. 4 (Boston, MA: Brill, 2018), 6.
3 Ibid.
4 Ibid., 49.
5 Russell D. Moore, *Adopted for Life: The Priority of Adoption for Christian Families & Churches* (Wheaton, IL: Crossway Books, 2009), loc 730, Kindle.
6 Ibid.
7 Ibid., loc 205.
8 Ibid., loc 710.
9 Ibid., loc 224.
10 Swinton and Brock, *A Graceful Embrace*, 438.
11 Ibid., 439.
12 Ibid.
13 A. A. Hoekema, *Saved by Grace* (Grand Rapids, MI: William B. Eerdmans Publishing Company, 1994), 186.
14 Dockery, *Holman Concise Bible Commentary*, Romans 8:23.
15 https://onlinelibrary-wiley-com.seu.idm.oclc.org/journal/15406385.
16 Ibid., 329.
17 Michael J. Gorman, *Becoming the Gospel: Paul, Participation, and Mission* (Grand Rapids, MI: William B. Eerdmans Publishing Company, 2015), 52.
18 Kenneth Numfor Ngwa, "Ethnicity, Adoption, and Exodus: A Socio-Rhetorical Reading of Exodus 2:1-10," *Journal for the Study of the Old Testament* 38, no. 2 (December 2013): 185.
19 http://www.sbts.edu/family/2014/04/16/equipping-the-generations-adoption-is-bigger-than-you-think/.
20 Ibid., 73.

Chapter 10: Historical Status of Orphans

1 Swinton and Brock, *A Graceful Embrace*, 41.
2 Ibid., 42.
3 Ibid., 43.
4 Ibid., 45.
5 Ibid., 42.
6 Ibid., 43.
7 Graham Fitzpatrick, "Killing Newborns in Ancient Greece and Rome," *Internet Bible College*, last modified 2006, accessed May 22, 2017, http://internetbiblecollege.net/Lessons/Killing%20Newborns%20In%20Ancient%20Greece%20And%20Rome.htm
8 Harold Bennett, "The Exposure of Infants in Ancient Rome," *The Classical Journal* 18, no. 6 (1923): 341, accessed May 23, 2017, http://www.jstor.org/stable/3288906.
9 Fitzpatrick, "Killing Newborns in Ancient Greece and Rome, Pdf, 2006," 1.
10 Carlos Sánchez-Moreno Ellart, "Homicide in Rome," *The Encyclopedia of Ancient History* (2012): 1, accessed May 23, 2017, http://doi.wiley.com/10.1002/9781444338386.wbeah13112.
11 Naomi J. Norman, "Death and Burial of Roman Children: The Case of the Yasmina Cemetery at Carthage-Part II, The Archaeological Evidence," *Mortality* 8, no. 1 (February 2003): 38, accessed May 23, 2017, http://www.tandfonline.com/doi/abs/10.1080/1357627021000063115.
12 N. S. Gill, "Exposure of Infants Was Near Universal," Thoughtco, accessed March 9, 2019, https://www.thoughtco.com/roman-exposure-of-infants-118370.
13 Ibid.
14 Ibid.
15 Max Radin, "The Exposure of Infants in Roman Law and Practice," *The Classical Journal* 20, no. 6 (1925): 339, accessed May 23, 2017, http://www.jstor.org/stable/3288457.
16 Michael Oblanden, "From Right to Sin: Laws on Infanticide in Antiquity," *Neonatology* 109, no. 1 (2015): 56, Karger, accessed May 22, 2017, https://www.karger.com/Article/PDF/440875.
17 Odd Magne Bakke, *When Children Became People: The Birth of Childhood in Early Christianity* (Minneapolis, MN: Fortress Press, 2005), 55.
18 Oblanden, "From Right to Sin," 57.
19 Ibid., 59.
20 Ray Laurence, "Why Were New Born Children Left to Die in Ancient Rome?" University of Kent, 2016, accessed May 23, 2017, https://blogs.

kent.ac.uk/lucius-romans/2016/06/15/why-were-new-born-children-left-to-die-in-ancient-rome/.

21 Ibid.

22 John Eastburn Boswell, "Expositio and Oblatio: The Abandonment of Children and the Ancient and Medieval Family," *The American Historical Review* 89, no. 1 (February 1984): 15, accessed May 25, 2017, http://www.jstor.org/stable/10.2307/1855916?origin=crossref.

23 Ibid.

24 Mindy Nichols, "Did Ancient Romans Love Their Children? Infanticide in Ancient Rome" (Master's Thesis, Western Oregon University, Monmouth, OR, 2008), 19.

25 Oblanden, "From Right to Sin," 60.

26 Ibid.

27 Boswell, "Expositio and Oblatio," 12.

28 Ibid.

29 Ibid.

30 Fitzpatrick, "Killing Newborns in Ancient Greece and Rome," 1.

31 Ibid., 4.

32 Ibid.

33 Stephen Bigger, "The Exposure of Infants among Jews and Christian in Antiquity," *Journal for the Study of the Old Testament* 35, no. 5 (June 2011): 66.

34 Boswell, "Expositio and Oblatio," 17.

35 Ibid., 20.

36 Ibid., 21.

37 Ibid., 27.

38 Ibid., 28.

39 Mark Golden, "Did the Ancients Care When Their Children Died?," *Greece and Rome (Second Series)* 35, no. 02 (1988): 160, accessed June 2, 2017, http://journals.cambridge.org/article_S0017383500033064.

40 Gill, "Exposure of Infants Was Near Universal," 1.

41 Joanie Gruber, "Orphan Care in The Early Church: A Heritage to Recapture" (presented at the North American Association of Christians in Social Work Convention 2011, Pittsburgh, PA, October 21, 2011).

42 Darin Duane Lenz, "Strengthening the Faith of the Children of God: Pietism, Print, and Prayer in the Making of a World Evangelical Hero, George Muller of Bristol (1805-1898)" (PhD diss., Kansas State University, Manhattan, KS 2010), 2. Kansas State University, accessed January 24, 2023, https://krex.k-state.edu/dspace/handle/2097/3880.

43 Marcy Kay Wilson, "Dear Little Living Arguments: Orphans and Other Poor Children, Their Families, and Orphanages, Baltimore and Liverpool, 1840-1910" (Ph.D. diss., University of Maryland, College Park, 2009), 3. University of Maryland, accessed January 24, 2023, https://drum.lib.

umd.edu/bitstream/handle/1903/9924/Wilson_umd_0117E_10884.pdf?sequence=1&isAllowed=y.

44 Ibid., 377.

45 Lyanne Candy Ruff, "Thrown on the Cold Charity of the World: Kansas Cares for Its Orphans, 1859-1919" (PhD? diss., University of Kansas, Lawrence, Kansas, 2012), 48.

46 Ibid., 49.

47 Ibid., 115.

48 James Fremont Richardson, "A Mission for Orphans in the Lutheran Church-Missouri Synod: A Brief History of the Martin Luther Orphans' Home at Brook Farm, West Roxbury, MA (1871-1945)," *Concordia Historical Institute Quarterly* 67, no. 4 (1994): 185.

49 Ibid., 188.

50 Bill Hancock and Johan Mostert, *CompaCare Compassion Care System Workbook* (Hot Springs, AR: Compact Family Service, 2017), 1.

51 Ibid., 18.

52 Mark Deymaz, *Disruption: Repurposing the Church to Redeem the Community* (Nashville TN: Thomas Nelson, 2017), 659.

Chapter 11: Current Status of Foster Care

1 Annie E. Casey Foundation, "Child Welfare and Foster Care Statistics."

2 Ibid.

3 Ibid.

4 Jean D'Amico, Kelvin Pollard, and Alicia VanOrman, *2018 Kids Count Data Book: State Trends in Child Well-Being* (Baltimore, MD: Annie E. Casey Foundation, 2018), accessed October 21, 2018, https://www.aecf.org/resources/2018-kids-count-data-book/.

5 Neil Post, *The Disappearance of Childhood* (New York: Vintage Books, Random House, 1994), loc. 85, Kindle.

6 Ibid., loc. 76.

7 Ibid., loc. 91.

8 Ibid., loc. 81.

9 Ibid., loc. 132.

10 Ibid., loc. 1084.

11 Ibid., loc. 1893.

12 Ibid., loc. 1953.

13 Ibid., loc. 1969.

14 Ibid., loc. 2318.

15 Bowley and Franklin, *Make It Zero*, 24.

16 Craig Benson, "U.S. Poverty Rate is 12.8% but Varies Significantly by Age," United States Census Bureau, October 4, 2022, accessed April 3, 2023, https://www.census.gov/library/stories/2022/10/poverty-rate-varies-by-age-groups.html.
17 Ibid., 40.
18 Ibid., 89.
19 Ibid., 98.
20 Swinton and Brock, *Graceful Embrace*, 4:43.
21 Ibid., 444.
22 Matthew LeClaire, "Foster Care in Reno Nevada: Does Aging-Out of Foster Care Increase the Presence of Risk Factors and Criminality?" (Master's thesis, University of Nevada, Reno, 2014), 55. Scholar Works, accessed January 24, 2023, https://scholarworks.unr.edu/bitstream/handle/11714/2371/LeClaire_unr_0139M_11650.pdf?sequence=1&isAllowed=y.
23 Ibid.
24 Erica Newman, "History of Transracial Adoption: A New Zealand Perspective," *American Indian Quarterly* 37, no. 1-2 (2013): 246.
25 Ibid., 250.
26 Jane E. Schooler, Betsy Keefer Smalley, and Timothy J. Callahan, *Wounded Children Healing Homes: How Traumatized Children Impact Adoptive and Foster Families* (Colorado Springs, CO: Nav Press, 2009), 93, Kindle.
27 Ibid., loc. 109.
28 Ibid., loc. 863.
29 Ibid., loc. 236.
30 Ibid., loc. 911.
31 Ibid., loc. 2889.
32 Purvis, Cross, and Sunshine, *Connected Child*, loc. 3129.

PART FOUR: GETTING INVOLVED

1 Forbes and Post, *Beyond Consequences*, 96.
2 Ibid., loc. 49.
3 Ibid.
4 Ibid., loc. 96.
5 Mary Frances Bowley and Jennifer Bradley Franklin, *Make It Zero: The Movement to Safeguard Every Child* (Chicago, IL: Moody Publishers, 2016), 15.
6 Ibid., 16.
7 Moore, *Adopted for Life*, loc. 220, Kindle.
8 Ibid.
9 Purvis, Cross, and Sunshine, *Connected Child*, loc. 269, Kindle.
10 Ibid., loc 265.

11 Ibid., loc. 273.
12 Ibid., loc. 250.
13 Ibid., loc. 250.

Chapter 12: CompaCare Foster Family Support

1 Westerlund, "Adoption as Spiritual Praxis in Individualized Times," 327.
2 Bob Smietana, "Adoption, Foster Care, Commonplace in Churches." *LifeWay*, January 24, 2018, accessed March 21, 2019, https://lifewayresearch.com/2018/01/24/adoption-foster-care-commonplace-in-churches/.
3 Ibid.
4 Jill C. Schreiber and Michael J. Culbertson, "Religious Socialization of Youth Involved in Child Welfare," *Child Abuse & Neglect* 38, no. 7 (July 2014): 1209, accessed October 14, 2018, https://linkinghub.elsevier.com/retrieve/pii/S0145213414001318.
5 Hancock and Mostert, *CompaCare Compassion Care System Manual*, 41.
6 Ibid., 46.
7 *National Foster Care and Family Restoration Ministry Model* (Hot Springs, AR: AGFSA and FaithBridge Foster Care, February 2013), 8.
8 Ibid.
9 Moore, *Adopted for Life*, loc. 220.
10 Ibid.
11 Ibid., loc. 2825.
12 Ibid., loc. 2834.
13 Purvis, Karyn B., David R. Cross, and Wendy Lyons Sunshine. *The Connected Child: Bring Hope and Healing to Your Adoptive Family*. New York: McGraw-Hill Publishers, 2007. Kindle loc 286.
14 Matthew Scott Thompson, "Adoption Rates Among Evangelicals: A Mixed Methods Study" (Ed.D. diss., Southern Baptist Theological Seminary, Louisville, KY, 2015), 81.

Chapter 13: Local Church Pilot: Program

1 Annie E. Casey Foundation, "Child Welfare and Foster Care Statistics."
2 Hancock and Mostert, *CompaCare Compassion Care System Manual*, 8.
3 *Wisconsin Department of Children and Families Out-of-Home Report 2016*, Data Source: dWiSACWIS: Division of Safety and Permanence, 2018.
4 Bill Hancock, "CompaCare Training Presentation" (Training, Compact Family Service, Hot Springs, AR, September 25, 2017).
5 Jason Johnson, interview by Robert Griffith, March 1, 2016.

6 "Safe Families," *Safe Families*, accessed November 24, 2016, http://safe-families.org/.
7 See https://www.project127.com/.
8 Carla Barnhill, "Churches Adopt Adoption: Project 1:27," *ChristianityToday.com*, accessed November 24, 2016, http://www.christianitytoday.com/ct/2010/july/11.23.html.
9 Ted Stackpole, interview by Robert Griffith, April 10, 2018.
10 Hancock and Mostert, *CompaCare Compassion Care System Manual*, 8.
11 Ibid., 22.
12 Ibid., 26.
13 Ibid., 27.
14 Hancock and Mostert, *CompaCare Compassion Care System Manual*, 8.
15 Hancock and Mostert, *CompaCare Compassion Care System Manual*, 8 .
16 Ron Rodgers and Michael Graveley, interview, Kenosha, WI, September 13, 2017.
17 Samantha Kerkman, "Speaker's Task Force on Foster Care," November 30, 2017, http://legis.wisconsin.gov/2017/committees/assembly/fc/statistics/.
18 Ibid.
19 Ibid.
20 Ibid.
21 Ibid.
22 Jason Rossell, interview by Robert Griffith, January 19, 2018.
23 Michelle Lang, interview by Robert Griffith, March 2, 2018.
24 Michael Graveley, interview by Robert Griffith, March 8, 2018.
25 Ibid.
26 Ibid.

Chapter 14: Local Church Pilot: Evaluation

1 Bill Hancock, interview by Robert Griffith, October 1, 2017.
2 Bill Hancock, "Assemblies of God CompaCare Training."
3 Ron Rogers, interview by Robert Griffith, February 17, 2017.

Conclusion

1 "4 Statistics You Should Know about the Orphan Crisis."
2 "Children Aging out of Foster Care."
3 Cruver, "Adoption Is Bigger than You Think," 73.
4 Oswalt, *The NIV Application Commentary: Isaiah*, 78.
5 Bullock, *An Introduction to the Old Testament Prophetic Books*, 161.
6 Flesher, "Mercy Triumphs," 183.

7 Allen, "Renewal of the Christian Community," 305.

8 Swinton and Brock, *A Graceful Embrace*, 46.

9 Ibid.

10 Moore, *Adopted for Life*, loc. 205.

11 Ibid., loc. 710.

12 Ibid., loc. 224.

13 Naomi Steinberg, *The World of the Child in the Hebrew Bible* (Sheffield S3 7QB: Sheffield Phoenix Press, 2015), 124.

14 Ibid.

Printed in the USA
CPSIA information can be obtained
at www.ICGtesting.com
LVHW090101071123
763210LV00003B/6